SIMPLY
KNITTED
SOCKS

SIMPLY KNITTED SOCKS

30 BEAUTIFUL PATTERNS TO CREATE

CHRISTINE BOGGIS

CONTENTS

Royal Bed Socks 14

Sleepy Socks 16

Cosy Bed Socks 18

New Baby Gift Set 30

Lavender Lace Booties 48

Citrus Stripe 52

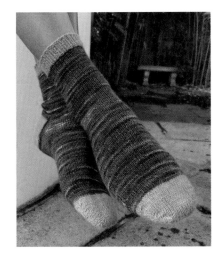

Major Tom's Socks 60

Mary 88

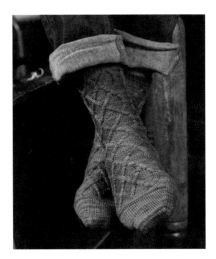

Something Blue for the Groom 106

STEP INTO SOCK KNITTING

Dip your toe into this addictive woolly world

Sock knitting is a rite of passage for knitters. To the uninitiated it may look daunting and unachievable: What are all those needles for? How do you turn a heel? Is it appropriate to keep talking about gussets? But for those in the know, socks are the perfect project: they are quick, portable, can be adapted from the most basic TV knitting to really stimulating challenges, and are interesting from top to toe – or the other way around.

There are so many different sections to a sock that even with a vanilla stocking stitch version you're never far from a good bit: if you're starting at the top you've got your stretchy cuff, your interesting (or relaxing) leg pattern, then the heel flap or straight to the heel turn, followed by the foot – with or without a gusset – and before you can get bored of that, you're on to the toe decreases.

From the toe up you start with just a few stitches and increase until you have the right number, then practise your main pattern on the foot before turning the heel and working the leg pattern. Once you get to the cuff you're on the home stretch.

This book aims to introduce you to sock knitting the easy way, with some super-quick chunky bed sock patterns and a whole collection of swift and cute baby booties that make perfect presents for new arrivals. These simple sections will introduce you to most of the techniques you need to know for any sock knitting – or you can plunge right in with the more standard sock patterns in the third part of the book, many of which are simple enough to make a brilliant first sock knit.

There is a photographic techniques section at the back of the book, so as a beginner you should be able to pick any pattern and find all the resources you need to knit it. The only limit is your own patience: a heavily cabled design in a thin 4 ply wool will take considerably longer than a chunky bed sock or a stripy baby bootie.

SECOND SOCK SYNDROME

The only downside to sock knitting – if indeed you don't consider this a plus point – is that you have to knit two of the same thing. For many knitters this is a step too far, but there are plenty of ways to make it fun.

Experienced sock knitters will encourage you to cast on your second sock as soon as you finish the first – once it's on the needles it is much easier to return to and knit a few rounds. On the other hand, some recommend that you knit a range of single socks, then only knit the second ones when you need them – for a special occasion, a gift or whatever reason.

Recently I have started knitting my second sock the opposite way from the first – so if I knitted a toe-up sock, I will challenge myself to recreate it from the top down, such as in the *Sunshine Socks* on page 76. This is very straightforward with a simple heel turn or afterthought heel, but is just as possible with a heel flap and gusset – although it will involve a bit of maths and ingenuity.

It is also possible to knit two socks at the same time using a long circular needle and the magic loop method – find out how on page 140. Finally, you could just buck society's expectations and knit single socks – who says they have to match? If someone asks you why your socks don't match, just ask them why theirs do.

I hope you enjoy this book and find yourself loving sock knitting as much as I do – let's face it, it's a proper addiction and if I don't have a sock on my needles as one of my works in progress, I just don't feel right. So step in and get knitting!

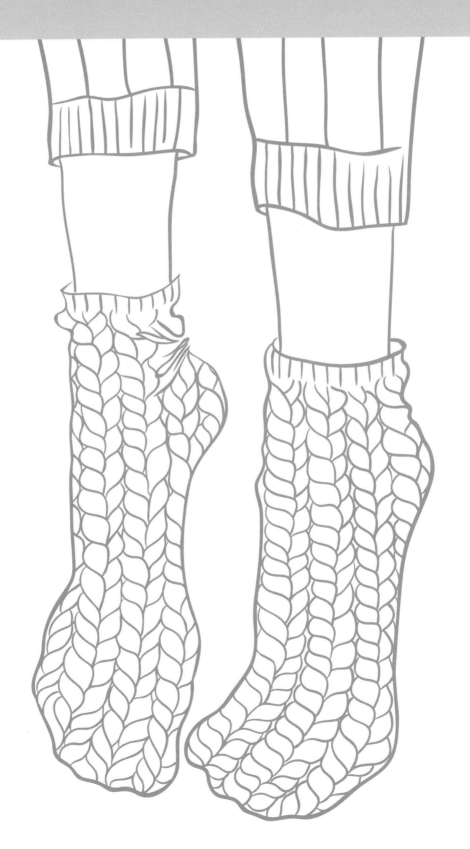

HOW TO KNIT SOCKS

The knitty gritty of your footwear's component parts

Socks are usually – always in this book – knitted in one of two ways: from the cuff down, or from the toe up. Some socks have a heel flap and gusset, others a simpler turned heel. Most patterns can be adapted from one method to another with a little bit of ingenuity – so feel free to mix and match at will.

CUFF

The cuff's main aim is to be stretchy – to allow you to get your foot into the sock and then to hold it up once it's on. If you're casting on at the cuff, use a method that is stretchy but firm, as you would for a neckline or jumper cuffs. The long-tail method is perfect. If you're casting off here, you're looking for stretch too – two types of stretchy cast off are detailed on pages 145 and 146. The standard cast off (see page 144) doesn't usually have enough give for a sock, so if you want to use it try doing it with a larger needle to make it more flexible.

LEG

This is where the real magic happens – an all-around pattern adorns the part of your sock most people will see.

HEEL

There are two main types of heel: a simple heel turn, in which short rows are worked for the whole heel, and a heel flap and gusset, which adds extra shaping to the sock and is perfect for people with high insteps. Both types of heel can be worked from the top down or the toe up. Heel flaps are exactly what they sound like – a simple straight flap worked back and forth downwards from one side of the leg. It can be worked in a

simple stocking stitch, used for extra patterning or worked with a slip stitch pattern that will add strength to this crucial part of the sock anatomy.

Simple heels can also use different colours or stitch patterns for extra contrast – a simple reverse stocking stitch heel can be surprisingly effective. When working a top-down heel flap and gusset, stitches are decreased at the heel turn, then picked up along the sides of the heel flap.

Heels are turned using short rows, which means you work back and forth over fewer stitches each time you turn, creating a wedge shape. When working a simple heel you will then work back over your short rows, working over more stitches each time you turn until you return to the full stitch count. For a heel flap design you will only work one half of the short row section as the second half is provided by the heel flap.

There are various techniques you can use to avoid holes when you turn in the middle of a row. My two favourites are shadow-wrap short rows (see page 132) and German short rows (page 133). These can be used interchangeably or swapped for your own favourite short row method – in each pattern I have detailed where to wrap and turn and noted which method I used, but feel free to work as you wish.

GUSSET

This is the name given to the section where the sock decreases from the heel to the main body of the foot, or increases from

the main body of the foot to the heel, depending on which way you are working. When working from the top down, after you have finished your heel flap and heel turn, usually ending with a reduced number of stitches across the heel, you will pick stitches up on one side of the heel flap, pattern across the instep, then pick up stitches down the second side of the heel flap to return to working in the round. These picked up stitches are usually worked through the back loop on the next round, and once you have all the stitches in play you decrease until you reach the final stitch count to create the gusset shaping (see page 131).

When working from the toe up, you will start the gusset shaping around the middle of the foot and increase on either side of the instep stitches until you have the required number of stitches. Then you turn the heel and continue working back and forth, working the last heel stitch together with the first gusset stitch on each row, until you reach the final stitch count and continue in the round for the leg (see page 134).

FOOT

This section is nearly as good as the leg – or better, depending on your perspective: if you've worked from the top down, you'll find your foot goes much quicker than your leg because you're working half your stitches in stocking stitch for the sole. If you're working from the toe up you'll have a nice easy start to get you going before you get into the really meaty bit of the leg later on. Some designers feature patterns on the soles of their socks, but I worry that you'll end up with funny marks on your feet, so mine are all plain vanilla stocking stitch or a simple slip stitch pattern for extra strength.

TOE

The toes in these sock patterns are all fairly similar: if you're working from the top down you will decrease to a certain point, then graft the remaining stitches together to finish (see page 142). If you're working from the toe up, you'll cast on using Judy's Magic Cast On (see page 116), then increase until you have the correct stitch count for the foot. Other cast ons are available, but this one is my favourite.

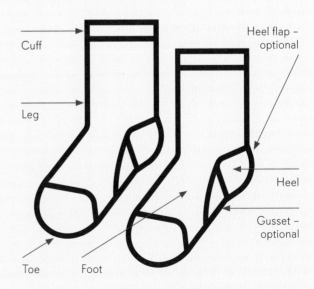

Cuff

Leg

Toe   Foot

Heel flap – optional

Heel

Gusset – optional

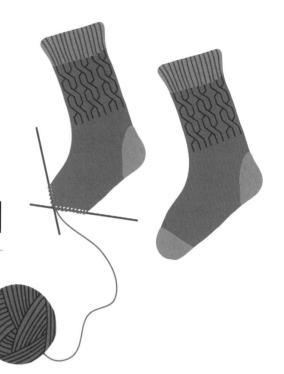

SOCK YARNS: THE LOWDOWN

What makes a perfect sock yarn?

Check out our top tips here

The first pair of socks I ever knitted were in a beautiful, hand-dyed, Merino-like pure wool that was as soft as cashmere. They were wonderful. I wore them again and again – but within a few weeks the section of sole under my heel had melted away, and the part under the balls of my feet was transparent.

The hard lesson I learnt was that sock yarns need to be hardwearing. The traditional way to strengthen them is to add in some synthetic fibre, such as nylon – so a standard 4 ply sock yarn will be a blend of 75% wool and 25% nylon. But there are other ways.

As our planet faces a crisis of plastic pollution, many knitters are looking for synthetic-free yarns, and there are plenty of options. You can find natural blends that add strength without including plastic, such as Onion's Nettle Sock Yarn, and brands including The Fibre Co and Isager have released sock yarns made using recycled nylon. Many of the projects in this book are designed using standard sock yarns. Those that are made from pure natural fibres are for socks that are not meant for a great deal of hiking – like bed socks and baby booties.

Swapping yarns is easy – 4 ply sock yarn is a fairly regular size across the board, so feel free to swap any of those for a yarn from your stash, a hand-dyed favourite or a plastic-free alternative. A 100g ball or skein should be plenty for an adult-size pair. For other weights, such as chunky-knitted bed socks, I recommend the website yarnsub.com – and take care to swatch and check the metreage when making a substitution.

CARING FOR YOUR HAND KNITS

Always read the yarn band carefully before you wash your hand knits – and always wash a swatch before laundering a painstakingly made garment. Many sock yarns are made to be machine-washable and may even tolerate a 40°C wash – but I tend to wash mine on the hand-wash cycle in the machine.

For more delicate fibres, soak in lukewarm water with a gentle wool wash. Squeeze out excess water, then roll your knit in a towel and step on it to squeeze out some more. Never wring your knits. Dry flat.

Some of these patterns recommend blocking. You can get dedicated sock blockers which are great if you're planning on knitting a lot of them – otherwise, a folded up towel and a few pins will do. Make sure your pins are in a metal that won't rust, as this would stain your socks. To block, slightly moisten your knit, pin it out or place it on the sock blocker, then cover with a damp cloth (I use muslins left over from when my kids were babies, but tea towels work just as well) and leave until completely dry.

PLEASE NOTE

In all these patterns, yarn amounts given are based on average requirements and are approximate.

TOOLS OF THE TRADE

The socks in this book are all knitted in the round, so you can work them either on double-pointed needles or on circular needles, using the magic loop method.

DOUBLE-POINTED NEEDLES

My favourite way to knit socks is using a set of five double-pointed needles or dpns. My stitches are spread across four needles and I work each set of stitches using a fifth needle. For smaller circumferences such as the toe I go down to three needles. Dpns come in a variety of materials but my favourite for sock knitting are 6in (15cm)-long metal needles. Because needles for sock knitting are often very fine, it is easy to snap wooden ones if you accidentally sit on them.

CIRCULAR NEEDLES

Like dpns these come in materials including wood, metal, carbon fibre, plastic and more. They can either be fixed, or part of a set of interchangeable needles in different sizes. Some brands offer specialist interchangeable needles for sock knitting, but standard circulars can be used for socks and many other things.

SCISSORS

Sharp scissors are essential for sock knitting as you will often be using a yarn strengthened with nylon or another synthetic fibre that you can't snap easily by hand.

SEWING NEEDLES

Use large-eyed, blunt-ended sewing needles for grafting and weaving in ends.

STITCH MARKERS

Stitch markers are essential for keeping track of where you are when knitting in the round. In most of the patterns in this book you will place a marker on the needle at the beginning of the round and one at the halfway point.

CABLE NEEDLE

A small double-pointed needle is used to create cable designs in some of the sock patterns in this book. They come in different shapes and sizes – just make sure yours is small enough to work with your knitting needles. If you don't have a cable needle small enough, a spare dpn will work just as well.

MEASURING TAPE

Keep track of where you are with a measuring tape – it can be handy to have both centimetres and inches marked, and there are plenty of small portable tapes available for crafters.

QUICK AND COSY

Try out your sock knitting
skills with these swift
projects in soft and
chunky yarns

13

ROYAL BED SOCKS

Feel like a queen on cold nights with these quick and cosy chunky socks, sized from tiny tots to grown-ups for the perfect Mummy-and-me look.

SIZE

To fit: 1yr[2-3yrs:4-6yrs: women's (approx size 7)]
Foot circumference: 6[6:8:9½]in (15[15:20:24]cm)
Foot length: 4[6¼:8:11]in (10[16:20:28]cm)
Figures in square brackets refer to larger sizes: where there is only one set of figures this applies to all sizes.

YOU WILL NEED

Erika Knight Maxi Wool
100% wool (approx 88yd/80m per 100g)
1 x 100g ball in Manga 214
3 x 10mm double-pointed needles

TENSION

9 sts x 12 rows to 4in (10cm) over st st.
Use larger or smaller needles if necessary to obtain correct tension.

PATTERN NOTES

These socks are knitted from the toe up, cast on using Judy's Magic Cast On (page 116). The heel is turned using shadow-wrap short rows (page 132) and the cuff is cast off using the stretchy method (page 145). The socks can be adjusted to fit any size foot, but you will need more yarn if you increase the largest size.

SOCK (MAKE 2)

Cast on 6 sts using 2 dpns and Judy's Magic Cast On. Pm to mark beg of rnd and after 3 sts to mark halfway point.
Rnd 1: (K1, m1, k1, m1, k1) twice (10 sts).
Rnd 2: (K1, m1, k to last st before m, m1, k1) twice (14 sts).
Rep rnd 2 another 0[0:1:2] times.
14[14:18:22] sts.

SET MOSS STITCH

Rnd 1: K1[1:1:2], (p1, k1) 3 times, p0[0:1:1], k to end.
Rnd 2: K2[2:2:3], (p1, k1) 3 times, k to end.
Rep rnds 1 and 2 until foot meas 2½[4:4¾:7½]in (6[10:12:19]cm) or 1½[2¼:3¼:4]in (4[6:8:9]cm) less than desired length, ending with rnd 1.

TURN HEEL

Short row 1 (RS): Work as rnd 2 to last 2 sts, sl1, w&t.

Short row 2 (WS): Sl1, p to last 2 sts, sl1, w&t.
Short row 3: Sl1, k to 2 sts before wrapped st, sl1, w&t.
Short row 4: Sl1, p to 2 sts before wrapped st, sl1, w&t.
Rep short rows 3 and 4 another 1[2:3:4] times.
Short row 5 (RS): K to first wrapped st, k wrap tog with wrapped st, turn.
Short row 6 (WS): K to first wrapped st, k wrap tog with wrapped st, turn.
Rep short rows 5 and 6 until all wraps have been worked, then k to end.

CUFF

Rib rnd: P0[0:0:1], (k1, p1) to end[end:end:last st], k0[0:0:1].
Rep rib rnd until cuff meas 2½[3:4¾:5½]in (6[8:12:14]cm) or desired length.
Cast off using a stretchy cast off.

TO FINISH

Weave in ends.

SLEEPY SOCKS

Lace looks really striking in a super chunky yarn and this is a great quick project to try out both lace and sock-knitting techniques.

SIZE
To fit: Average woman
Cuff circumference: 8in (20cm)
Foot length: 9¾in (24.5cm) (adjustable)

YOU WILL NEED
Rowan Cocoon 80% wool, 20% mohair (approx 126yd/115m per 100g)
1 x 100g ball in 851 Misty Rose
7mm double-pointed or circular needles
Stitch markers
Scrap yarn

PATTERN NOTE
These socks are knitted from the toe up. They are cast on using Judy's Magic Cast On (page 116), the heel is an afterthought heel (page 126) and the cuff is cast off using the stretchy method (page 145).

TENSION
12 sts and 16 rnds to 4in (10cm) over st st.
Use larger or smaller needles if necessary to obtain correct tension.

LACE PATTERN
Worked over 10 sts and 4 rnds
Rnd 1: K1, ssk, k1, yo, k2, yo, k1, k2tog, k1.
Rnds 2 and 4: K4, p2, k4.
Rnd 3: Ssk, k1, yo, k4, yo, k1, k2tog.
These 4 rnds form patt and are repeated.

SOCK (MAKE 2)
Cast on 12 sts using Judy's Magic Cast On.
Rnd 1: Knitting any twisted sts tbl to untwist them, work as foll: pm to mark beg of rnd, k6, pm to mark halfway point, k to end.
Rnd 2 (inc): *K1, m1, k to 1 st before m, m1, k1; sm, rep from * to end (16 sts).
Rnd 3: Knit, slipping markers.
Rep rnds 2 and 3 until you have 28 sts, ending with rnd 3.
SET FOOT PATTERN
Rnd 1: K1, p1, work rnd 1 of Lace Patt

CHART

10	9	8	7	6	5	4	3	2	1	
				•	•					4
/		O					O		\	3
				•	•					2
		/		O		O		\		1
10	9	8	7	6	5	4	3	2	1	

once, p1, k1, sm, k to end.
This rnd sets position of Lace Patt with 2 rib sts on each side and a st st sole.
Cont as set, rep rnds 1-4 of Lace Patt 5 times in total, then rnds 1-3 once more.
Foot meas approx 8in (20cm) – or to approx 2in (5cm) less than desired length, ending with rnd 3.
SET AFTERTHOUGHT HEEL
Next rnd: Work patt rnd 4 as set to m, using scrap yarn k across rem sts. Return the 14 sts just worked to LH needle, then k across them again using working yarn.
Work 1 more rnd as set, working rnd 1 of Lace Patt.
Next rnd (dec): K1, p1, work rnd 2 of Lace Patt, p1, k1, sm, k6, k2tog, k to end (27 sts).
SET LEG PATTERN
Rnd 1: K1, p1, work rnd 3 of Lace Patt, p1, k1, sm, (p1, k1) to last st, p1.

KEY

☐	knit
•	purl
O	yo
\	ssk
/	k2tog

This rnd sets leg patt. Cont in Lace Patt and rib until you have worked a total of 11 reps of Lace Patt and Sock meas approx 13½in (34cm), or to ¾in (2cm) less than desired leg length, measured from scrap yarn to cuff.

SET CUFF
Next rnd: K1, p1, k2tog, (p1, k1) to last st, removing mid-rnd marker as you come to it, p1 (26 sts).
Work 1 more rnd in (k1, p1) rib.
Cast off in rib using a stretchy cast off.

WORK HEEL

Pick up 14 sts on either side of scrap yarn, then carefully remove it.
Pm to mark beg of rnd and after 7 sts to mark halfway point. Knit 1 rnd.
Rnd 1: *K1, ssk, k to 3 sts before m, k2tog, k1; sm, rep from * to end.
Rnd 2: Knit, slipping markers.
Rep rnds 1 and 2 until 12 sts rem.

TO FINISH

Graft heel sts together. Weave in ends.
Block to open out lace pattern.

COSY BED SOCKS

A super simple knit in a chunky British wool, this would make a great first sock project.

SIZE
To fit: Average woman's foot
Ankle circumference: 8in (20cm)
Foot length (adjustable): 9in (23cm)

YOU WILL NEED
Erika Knight Maxi Wool 100% wool
(approx 88yd/80m per 100g)
2 x 100g hanks in Iced Gem
10mm double-pointed or circular needles

TENSION
9 sts and 12 rnds to 4in (10cm) over st st.
Use larger or smaller needles if necessary to obtain correct tension.

PATTERN NOTES
These socks are knitted from the toe up, cast on using Judy's Magic Cast On (page 116). The foot length is easily adjustable and the heel was turned using shadow-wrap short rows (page 132). The cuff was cast off using the stretchy method (page 145).

SOCK (MAKE 2)
Cast on 6 sts using Judy's Magic Cast On. Pm to mark beg of rnd and after 3 sts to mark halfway point. On first rnd work any twisted sts tbl to untwist them.
Rnd 1: (Kfb, k1, kfb) twice (10 sts).
Rnd 2: (K1, kfb, k to last 2 sts before m, kfb, k1) twice (14 sts).
Rep rnd 2 once more (18 sts).
Knit 1 rnd.
Rep last 2 rnds once more (22 sts).
SET GARTER SLIP ST PATT
Rnd 1: K1, (sl1, k3) twice, sl1, k to end.
Rnd 2: K2, (p3, k1) twice, k to end.
These 2 rnds set garter slip st patt on instep (11 sts) and 11 sts in st st for sole. Cont in patt until foot meas 7½in (19cm) or approx 2¾in (7cm) less than desired length, ending with rnd 1.
TURN HEEL
Short row 1 (RS): Patt rnd 2 to last st of rnd, w&t.
Short row 2 (WS): P to last sole st, w&t.
Short row 3: K to st before wrapped st, w&t.

Short row 4: P to st before wrapped st, w&t.
Rep short rows 3 and 4 twice more.
Short row 5 (RS): K to first wrapped st, k wrap tog with wrapped st, turn.
Short row 6 (WS): P to first wrapped st, p wrap tog with wrapped st, turn.
Rep last 2 rows until all wrapped sts have been worked tog with their wraps, then k to end of row.
LEG
Now cont in the rnd as foll:
Set-up rnd: K1, (sl1, k3) twice, (sl1, k2tog, k2) twice, sl1, k2.
Rnd 1: P1, (k1, p3) 4 times, k1, p3.
Rnd 2: K1, (sl1, k3) 4 times, sl1, k2.
Rep rnds 1 and 2 until leg meas 4¾in (12cm) or approx ¼in (1cm) less than desired length, ending with rnd 2.
Knit 1 rnd.
Cast off using a stretchy method.

TO FINISH
Weave in ends.

CABIN SOCKS

Ultra-soft and adorably chunky, these alpaca-blend socks are perfect for cabin and camping holidays, where they'll keep your toes toasty warm all night long.

SIZE
To fit: UK size 5-8
Cuff circumference: 8in (20cm)
Foot length (adjustable): 10½in (27cm)

YOU WILL NEED
Cascade Yarns Miraflores 80% alpaca, 20% nylon (approx 148yd/135m per 100g skein)
1 x 100g skein in 01 Walnut (A)
1 x 100g skein in 03 Almond (B)
5.5mm double-pointed or circular needles
Cable needle
Stitch markers

TENSION
14 sts and 20 rows to 4in (10cm) over st st.
Use larger or smaller needles if necessary to obtain correct tension.

PATTERN NOTES
These socks are knitted from the toe up, cast on using Judy's Magic Cast-On (page 116). The heel is turned using German short rows (page 133) and the cuff is cast off using the stretchy method (page 145).

CABLE PATTERN
Worked over 14 sts
Rnds 1 and 2: K2, p2, k6, p2, k2.
Rnd 3: K2, p2, C3B, C3F, p2, k2.
Rnd 4: As rnd 1.

SOCK (MAKE 2)
Using A and Judy's Magic Cast-On, cast on 8 sts. Pm to mark beg of rnd and after 4 sts to mark halfway point. Knit 1 rnd.
Next rnd: *Sm, k1, (kfb) twice, k1; rep from * once more (12 sts).
Next rnd: Knit.
Inc rnd: *Sm, k1, kfb, k to last 2 sts before m, kfb, k1; rep from * once more (inc 4).
Next rnd: Knit.

Rep last 2 rnds 3 more times (28 sts).
Knit 1 rnd.
Break off A and change to B.
Knit 1 rnd.

SET FOOT PATTERN
Referring to Chart or written instructions, work as foll:
Next rnd: Work row 1 of Cable Pattern, sm, k to end.
Work as set, repeating rows 1-4 of Cable Pattern, until you have 9 complete repeats or until foot meas 1½in (4cm) less than desired length.

TURN HEEL
Work in rev st st as foll:
Short row 1 (RS): Patt as set to halfway m, sm, p to last st, w&t.

CABLE PATTERN

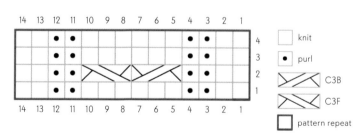

KEY

☐	knit
•	purl
⧄	C3B
⧅	C3F
☐	pattern repeat

Short row 2 (WS): K to last st, w&t.
Short row 3: P to last st before wrapped st, w&t.
Short row 4: K to last st before wrapped st, w&t.
Rep short rows 3 and 4 until 4 sts rem unwrapped at centre, ending after a WS row.
Short row 5 (RS): Sl1, p to first wrapped st, p wrap tog with wrapped st, turn.
Short row 6 (WS): Sl1, k to first wrapped st, k wrap tog with wrapped st, turn.
Rep short rows 5 and 6 until all wrapped sts have been worked, then cont in the rnd across all sts.
Next rnd: Patt as set.
SET LEG
Break off B and change to A.
Rib rnd: (K2, p2) around.
Rep rib rnd until leg meas 8¼in (21cm) from colour change.
Break A.
Using B, cast off using a stretchy method.

TO FINISH
Weave in ends.
Block if required.

JUMP! LEG WARMERS

Fashion goes around and comes around, so it's no surprise that 1970s and 1980s leg warmers are right back in fashion! This chunky pair features a chevron stripe.

SIZE
Cuff circumference: 10¼in (26cm)
Leg circumference: 12in (30cm)
Length: 13½in (34cm)

YOU WILL NEED
Rico Fashion Light Luxury 74% alpaca, 22% wool, 4% polyamide (approx 142yd/130m per 50g)
1 x 50g ball in 38 (A)
Rico Fashion Light Luxury Hand-Dyed 74% alpaca, 22% wool, 4% nylon (approx 137yd/125m per 50g)
1 x 50g ball in 07 (B)
5mm and 6mm double-pointed or circular needles
Stitch markers

TENSION
16 sts and 21 rnds to 4in (10cm) over Chevron Patt using 6mm needle.
Use larger or smaller needles if necessary to obtain correct tension.

PATTERN NOTES
These leg warmers are cast on using the long-tail method (page 113) and cast off loosely using standard cast off (page 144).

CHEVRON PATTERN
Worked over a multiple of 12 sts and 4 rnds
Rnd 1: K1, ssk, k3, yo, k1, yo, k3, k2tog.
Rnd 2: Knit.
Rnd 3: Rep row 1.
Rnd 4: Purl.

LEG WARMER (MAKE 2)
Using 5mm needles and A, cast on 48 sts. Join to work in the round, taking care not to twist sts, and pm to mark beg of rnd.
Rib rnd: (K1, p1) around.
Rep rib rnd 9 more times.
SET MAIN PATT
Change to 6mm needles.
Knit 1 rnd.

Change to B and work in Chevron Patt throughout, setting stripe patt as foll:
8 rnds B.
4 rnds A.
4 rnds B.
4 rnds A.
Rep the 20-rnd stripe patt once more, then work 8 more rnds in B.
Change to A.
Knit 1 rnd.
Change to 5mm needles.
Work rib rnd 10 times.
Cast off loosely.

TO FINISH
Weave in ends.
Block to open out lace pattern.

CHEVRON PATTERN

12	11	10	9	8	7	6	5	4	3	2	1	
•	•	•	•	•	•	•	•	•	•	•	•	4
/				O		O				\		3
												2
/			O			O				\		1
12	11	10	9	8	7	6	5	4	3	2	1	

KEY

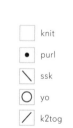

knit
• purl
\ ssk
O yo
/ k2tog

PITTER PATTER

Small projects are
perfect for trying out new
techniques – and baby
socks have the advantage
of being super cute and
perfect gifts to boot

TEENY WEENY TOE-UP TOASTIES

Baby socks are a fantastic way to try out new sock techniques before embarking on an adult project. Knitted in soft 4 ply Merino, these cute little toasties are designed to be worked on two double-pointed needles or using the magic loop method.

SIZE

To fit: Newborn[0-6:6-12:12-18]mths
Ankle circumference: 4[4:5:6]in (10[10:12.5:15]cm)
Foot length: 2¾[3¼:3½:4¼]in (7[8:9:10.5]cm)
Figures in square brackets refer to larger sizes: where there is only one set of figures this applies to all sizes.

YOU WILL NEED

MillaMia Naturally Soft Merino
100% Merino wool (approx 137yd/125m per 50g)
Small amounts in the following shades:
Blue contrast toe and heel sock:
164 Mist (A) and 106 Ink Blue (B)
Lilac and cream contrast toe and heel sock: 124 Snow (A) and 123 Lilac Blossom (B)
Grey and red wide stripy sock:
102 Storm (A) and 140 Scarlet (B)
White and pink narrow stripy sock:
125 Ice (A) and 122 Petal (B)
(Single sock weighs approx 5[5:10:10]g)
3.5mm double-pointed or circular needles
Stitch markers

TENSION

22 sts and 32 rows to 4in (10cm) over st st.
Use larger or smaller needles if necessary to obtain correct tension.

PATTERN NOTES

These socks are cast on using Judy's Magic Cast On (page 116), the heels are turned using shadow-wrap short rows (page 132) and the cuffs are cast off using the stretchy method (page 145).

CONTRAST HEEL AND TOE SOCK (MAKE 2)

*Cast on 14[14:18:22] sts in A using Judy's Magic Cast On.
Rnd 1: Pm to mark beg of rnd, k7[7:9:11], pm for halfway point, k to end.
Rnd 2 (inc): (Sm, k1, kfb, k to 2 sts before m, kfb, k1) twice.
Rnd 3: Knit.
Rep last 2 rnds 2[2:3:3] more times. 26[26:34:38] sts.
Change to B.*
Work without shaping for 12[14:17:22] rnds until Sock meas 2¼[2½:3:3¼]in (6[6.5:7.5:8.5]cm).

SHAPE HEEL

K across first half of sts, drop B but do not break yarn, join A and k to last st, w&t.
**Short row 1 (WS): P to last st before halfway point m, w&t.
Short row 2 (RS): K to 1 st before last wrapped st, w&t.
Short row 3: P to 1 st before last wrapped st, w&t.
Rep last 2 rows until 5[5:7:9] sts rem unwrapped, ending with a WS row.
Short row 4 (RS): K to first wrapped st, k wrapped st tog with wrap, turn.
Short row 5 (WS): P to first wrapped st, p wrapped st tog with wrap, turn.
Rep last 2 rows until all wrapped sts have been worked.**
K to halfway m, break A, join B and k to end of rnd.

LEG

Cont in B for 5[9:10:12] rnds. Break B.

CUFF

Using A, work 5 rnds in k1, p1 rib.
Cast off using a stretchy cast off.

TO FINISH

Weave in ends.

WIDE STRIPY SOCK (MAKE 2)

Work as for Contrast Socks from * to *.

SET STRIPES

Work 2 rnds in B, 3 rnds in A.

***Cont in stripe patt without shaping until 12[14:17:22] rnds have been worked from start of stripes. Sock meas 2¼[2½:3:3¼]in (6[6.5:7.5:8.5]cm).

SHAPE HEEL

Drop B but do not break yarn,

cont in A and work to last st, w&t.

Work as for Contrast Socks from ** to **.

LEG

Cont in stripe patt for 5[9:10:12] rnds.

CUFF

Using A, work 5 rnds in k1, p1 rib.

Cast off using a stretchy cast off.

TO FINISH

Weave in ends.

NARROW STRIPY SOCK (MAKE 2)

Work as for Contrast Socks from * to *.

SET STRIPES

Note: You may wish to use the helical stripes technique to avoid jogs (see page 136).

Work 1 row in B, 1 row in A.

Work as for Wide Stripy Socks from *** to end.

WALKING ON SUNSHINE BOOTIES

Bring a little sunshine into a new baby's life with these super-cute booties.

SIZES

To fit age: 6-12[12-24]mths
Cuff circumference: 4[4¾]in (10[12]cm)
Foot length: 3½[4¾]in (9[12]cm)
Figures in square brackets refer to larger sizes: where there is only one set of figures this applies to all sizes.

YOU WILL NEED

Cascade 220 Superwash Aran
100% Merino wool (approx 150yd/137.5m per 100g)
1 x 100g ball in 241 Sunflower
5mm double-pointed or circular needles
Stitch markers

TENSION

18 sts and 26 rnds to 4in (10cm) over rib.
15 sts and 24 rnds to 4in (10cm) over st st.
Use larger or smaller needles if necessary to obtain correct tension.

PATTERN NOTES

This toe-up design is cast on using Judy's Magic Cast On (page 116), the heel is turned using shadow-wrap short rows (page 132) and the cuff is cast off using the stretchy method (page 145).

SUNRISE PATTERN

Worked over 9 sts and 15 rows
Rnd 1: *K1, (k2tog, yo) twice, skpo, yo, k2.
Rnd 2 and all alt rnds: Knit.
Rnd 3: K1, p1, k2tog, yo, k1, yo, skpo, p1, k1.
Rnd 5: K2, p1, k1, yo, ssk, p1, k2.
Rnd 7: (K1, p1) 4 times, k1.
Rnd 9: (P1, k1) 4 times, p1.
Rnd 11: K1, (p1, k2) twice, p1, k1.
Rnd 13: (P1, k3) twice, p1.
Rnd 15: K4, p1, k4.

BOOTIE (MAKE 2)

Cast on 10 sts using Judy's Magic Cast On. Pm at beg and halfway point of rnd. On first rnd work any twisted sts tbl to untwist them.

SHAPE TOE

Inc rnd: *K1, kfb, k to last 2 sts before m, kfb, k1; sm, rep from * once (inc 4).
Rep inc rnd until you have 18[22] sts (9[11] each for instep and sole).
Knit 2 rnds.

SET SUNRISE PATTERN

Rnd 1: K0[1], work across rnd 1 of 9-st patt, k to end.

This rnd sets position of Sunrise Patt on instep and st st across sole.
Cont as set until all 15 rows have been worked.
Cont straight in st st until foot meas 3[4]in (7.5[10]cm).

TURN HEEL

Short row 1 (RS): K to last st, w&t.
Short row 2 (WS): P to 1 st before halfway point marker, w&t.
Short row 3: K to 1 st before wrapped st, w&t.
Short row 4: P to 1 st before wrapped st, w&t.
Rep rows 3 and 4 until 5 sts rem between wrapped sts, ending with a p row.
Short row 5 (RS): K to first wrapped st, k wrap tog with wrapped st, turn.
Short row 6 (WS): P to first wrapped st, p wrap tog with wrapped st, turn.
Rep last 2 rows until all wrapped sts have been worked tog with their wraps, k to end of rnd and cont in the rnd.

LEG

Rib rnd: (K1, p1) around.
Rep rib rnd until leg meas 3[4]in (7.5[10]cm).
Cast off.

TO FINISH

Weave in ends.

Sock is designed to be worn with leg folded over (see photos).

NEW BABY GIFT SET

Recycled cashmere is both sustainable and ultra-soft – the perfect fibre for a bootie and mitten gift set to greet a new arrival.

SIZE

To fit: Newborn or tiny baby
Mitten and bootie cuff circumference:
4¾in (12cm)
Mitten length: 2¾in (7cm)
Bootie length: 3in (8cm)

YOU WILL NEED

Rico Essentials Cashmere Recycled
DK 95% cashmere, 5% wool
(approx 77yd/70m per 25g)
1 x 25g ball in 004
3.5mm double-pointed needles
4 x 12in (30cm) lengths of 5mm ribbon
Tapestry needle with a large eye

TENSION

22 sts and 32 rnds to 4in (10cm)
over st st.
Use larger or smaller needles if
necessary to obtain correct tension.

PATTERN NOTE

These booties are knitted from the toe up and the mittens from the top down, using Judy's Magic Cast On (page 116). The heels are turned using shadow-wrap short rows (page 132) and the cuffs are cast off using the stretchy method (page 145).

MITTEN (MAKE 2)

**Cast on 12 sts using Judy's Magic Cast On. Pm to mark beg of rnd and after 6 sts to mark halfway point.
Rnd 1: Knit, working any twisted sts tbl to untwist them.
Increase rnd: *Kfb, k to last st before m, kfb; rep from * once more (16 sts).
Rep last rnd once more (20 sts).

SET MOSS STITCH INCREASES

Inc rnd: *Kfb, (k1, p1) to last st before m, kfb; rep from * once more (24 sts).**
Rep last rnd once more (28 sts).

SET MOSS STITCH

Rnd 1: (P1, k1) to end.
Rnd 2: (K1, p1) to end.
Rep last 2 rnds until Mitten meas 2¼in (5.5cm), ending with rnd 2.
Dec rnd: *K2tog, (p1, k1) to last 2 sts before m, k2tog; rep from * once more (24 sts).
Knit 2 rnds.
***Eyelet rnd:** (Yo, k2tog) to end.
Knit 2 rnds.
Purl 1 rnd.
Knit 1 rnd.
Rep last 2 rnds once more.
Cast off kwise using a stretchy cast off.

BOOTIE (MAKE 2)

Work as Mitten from ** to **.
Rep last rnd 2 more times (32 sts).

SET MOSS STITCH

Rnd 1: (P1, k1) to end.
Rnd 2: (K1, p1) to end.
Rep last 2 rnds until Bootie meas 2½in (6cm), ending with rnd 2.

TURN HEEL

Short row 1 (RS): Work as rnd 1 to last 2 sts, w&t.
Short row 2 (WS): (K1, p1) to last 2 sts before halfway marker, w&t.
Short rows 3 and 4: (P1, k1) to last 2 sts before wrapped sts, p1, w&t.
Keeping m st patt correct, rep short rows 3 and 4 until 6 sts rem unwrapped.
Short row 5 (RS): Patt to first wrapped st, patt wrapped st tog with wrap, turn.
Short row 6 (WS): Patt to first wrapped st, patt wrapped st tog with wrap, turn.
Rep short rows 5 and 6 until all wrapped sts have been picked up, then work over all sts in the rnd as foll:
Rnd 1: (K1, p1) to end.
Rnd 2: (P1, k1) to end.
Knit 4 rnds.
Work as Mitten from *** to end.

TO FINISH

Weave in ends.
Using a large-eyed tapestry needle, thread ribbon through the eyelets in Mittens and Booties, tie in a bow and trim ends.

STARS AND HEARTS BOOTIES

Simple textured motifs knitted in a worsted-weight yarn mean these super-soft booties make a perfect last-minute gift for a little one.

SIZE

To fit: Age 0-6[12-18:18-24]mths
Ankle circumference: 4[5:6]in (10[12.5:15]cm)
Foot length: 3½[4¼:4¾]in (9[10.5:12]cm)
Figures in square brackets refer to larger sizes: where there is only one set of figures this applies to all sizes.

YOU WILL NEED

Cascade Spuntaneous Worsted 100% extra-fine Merino wool (approx 208yd/190m per 100g) 15[20:25]g in 13 Blue Shadow (A)
Cascade Spuntaneous Worsted Effects 100% extra-fine Merino wool (approx 208yd/190m per 100g) 15[20:25]g in 305 Grey (B)
5mm double-pointed or circular needles
Stitch marker
Blunt-ended tapestry needle

TENSION

17 sts and 28 rnds to 4in (10cm) over st st.
Use larger or smaller needles if necessary to obtain correct tension.

PATTERN NOTES

These booties are knitted from the top down. They are cast on using the long-tail method (page 113) and joined in the round with a jogless join (page 115). The heel is turned using shadow-wrap short rows (page 132) and the toe stitches are grafted together to finish (page 142).

STAR BOOTIE (MAKE 2)

Using A, cast on 18[22:26] sts.
Join to work in the round, taking care not to twist sts. Pm to mark beg of rnd and after 9[11:13] sts for halfway point.

Rib rnd: (K1, p1) around.
Rep rib rnd until piece meas approx 2¼[2¾:3¼]in (6[7:8]cm).
Knit 1 rnd.

TURN HEEL

Short row 1 (RS): K8[10:12], w&t.
Short row 2 (WS): P to last st, w&t.
Short row 3: K to 1 st before wrapped st, w&t.
Short row 4: P to 1 st before wrapped st, w&t.
Rep rows 3 and 4 until 3 sts rem unwrapped.
Short row 5 (RS): K to wrapped st, k wrap tog with wrapped st, turn.

STAR CHART

HEART CHART

KEY

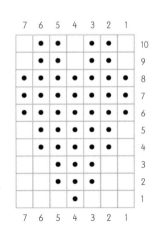

Short row 6 (WS): P to wrapped st, p wrap tog with wrapped st, turn.

Rep the last 2 rows until all wrapped sts have been worked, then k to end of rnd. Knit 2 rnds.

PLACE MOTIF

Rnd 1: K across sole sts to halfway m, sm, k1[2:3], work row 1 of Star Chart, k1[2:3].

This rnd places Chart.

Cont as set until Star Chart is complete.

SHAPE TOE

Dec rnd 1: *K1, ssk, k to last 3 sts before marker, k2tog, k1; sm, rep from * to end (dec 4).

Rep dec rnd until 10 sts rem.

Graft toe sts.

TO FINISH

Weave in ends.

HEART BOOTIE (MAKE 2)

Work as for Star Bootie, but using B and working from Heart Chart instead of Star Chart.

OLWEN SKYE

A hat and bootie set is the perfect gift to make sure a new arrival keeps nice and warm at both ends – and luxurious cashmere makes it an even lovelier present.

SIZES

To fit age: 0-6[6-12:12-18:18-24]mths
Brim circumference:
14½[16½:18½:20½]in (37[42:47:52]cm)
Bootie cuff circumference: 4[4¼:5:6]in
(10[11:12.5:15]cm)
Foot length: 2¾[3¼:3¾:4]in
(7[8.5:9.5:10.5]cm)
Figures in square brackets refer to larger sizes: where there is only one set of figures this refers to all sizes.

YOU WILL NEED

Debbie Bliss Luna 100% cashmere
(approx 82yd/75m per 25g)
1[1:2:2] x 25g balls in 08 Twilight (A)
1[2:2:2] x 25g balls in 03 Slate (B)
3.5mm double-pointed or circular needles
Stitch marker

TENSION

26 sts and 36 rnds to 4in (10cm)
over m st.
28 sts and 36 rnds to 4in (10cm)
over rib.
Use larger or smaller needles if necessary to obtain correct tension.

PATTERN NOTES

These booties are knitted from the toe up, cast on using Judy's Magic Cast On (page 116). The heel is turned using German short rows (page 133) and the cuff is cast off using the stretchy method (page 145). The hat is cast on using the long-tail method (page 113) and joined to work in the round with a jogless join (page 115).

BOOTIE (MAKE 2)

Using A and Judy's Magic Cast On, cast on 12 sts. Pm to mark beg of rnd and after 6 sts to mark halfway point.
Inc rnd: *K1, kfb, k to 2 sts before m, kfb, k1; sm, rep from * once more (inc 4).
Rep inc rnd 2 more times (24 sts).
Knit 1 rnd.
Rep last 2 rnds 1[2:3:4] times.
28[32:36:40] sts.
Change to B.
Next rnd: K2, (p1, k1) to last 2 sts before m, k2, sm, k to end.
Next rnd: K2, (k1, p1) to last 2 sts before m, k2, sm, k to end.
Rep these 2 rnds until foot meas 2¼[2½:2½:2¾]in (5.5[6.5:6.5:7]cm).

SHAPE HEEL

Short row 1 (RS): Patt to m, sm, k to last st, w&t.
Short row 2 (WS): P to last st before halfway m, w&t.
Short row 3: K to st before wrapped st, w&t.
Short row 4: P to st before wrapped st, w&t.
Rep short rows 3 and 4 until 6 sts rem unwrapped.
Short row 5 (RS): K to first wrapped st, k wrap tog with wrapped st, turn.
Short row 6 (WS): P to first wrapped st, p wrap tog with wrapped st, turn.
Rep short rows 5 and 6 until all wrapped sts have been worked, then k to end of rnd and knit 1 more rnd.

CUFF

Change to A.
Rib rnd: (K1, p1) around.
Rep rib rnd until cuff meas 2¼[2½:2½:2¾]in (5.5[6.5:6.5:7]cm).
Change to B.
Cast off using a stretchy cast off.

TO FINISH

Weave in ends.

HAT

Using B, cast on 96[108:120:132] sts.
Join to work in the round, taking care not
to twist sts, and pm to mark beg of rnd.
Change to A.

Rib rnd: (K1, p1) around.

Rep rib rnd until piece meas ½[½:¾:¾]in
(1[1:1.5:1.5]cm).

SET MOSS STITCH

Change to B.

Rnd 1: (P1, k1) around.

Rnd 2: (K1, p1) around.

Rep rnds 1 and 2 until piece meas
approx 3½[3½:4¼:4¼]in (9[9:11:11]cm).
Knit 1 rnd.

SHAPE CROWN

Change to A.

Knit 1 rnd.

Rnd 1: (K10, k2tog) around.
88[99:110:121] sts.

Rnd 2: Knit.

Rnd 3: (K9, k2tog) around.
80[90:100:110] sts.

Rnd 4: Knit.

Rnd 5: (K8, k2tog) around.
72[81:90:99] sts.

Rnd 6: Knit.

Rnd 7: (K7, k2tog) around.
64[72:80:88] sts.

Rnd 8: (K6, k2tog) around.
56[63:70:77] sts.

Rnd 9: (K5, k2tog) around.
48[54:60:66] sts.

Rnd 10: (K4, k2tog) around.
40[45:50:55] sts.

Rnd 11: (K3, k2tog) around.
32[36:40:44] sts.

Rnd 12: (K2, k2tog) around.
24[27:30:33] sts.

Rnd 13: (K1, k2tog) around.
16[18:20:22] sts.

Rnd 14: (K2tog) around. 8[9:10:11] sts.

Break yarn leaving a long tail and thread
through rem sts.

Pull tight to secure and fasten off.

TO FINISH

Weave in ends.

BO PEEP BOOTIES

A contrast heel and toe add that extra adorable factor
to these cute toe-up socks in a cosy broken rib pattern.

SIZE
To fit age: 0-6[6-12:12-18:18-24]mths
Bootie ankle circumference:
4[4¼:5:6]in (10[11:12.5:15]cm)
Foot length: 2¾[3¼:3¾:4]in
(7[8.5:9.5:10.5]cm)
*Figures in square brackets refer to larger
sizes: where there is only one set of
figures this applies to all sizes.*

YOU WILL NEED
West Yorkshire Spinners Bo Peep
Pure 100% Falkland Island wool
(approx 122yd/112m per 50g)
1 x 50g hank in 319 Blackcurrant (A)
1 x 50g hank in 010 Natural (B)
4mm circular or double-pointed needles
Stitch markers

TENSION
24 sts and 34 rnds to 4in (10cm)
over patt.
*Use larger or smaller needles if
necessary to obtain correct tension.*

PATTERN NOTES
These booties are knitted from the toe
up, cast on using Judy's Magic Cast On,
(page 116). The heel is turned using
shadow-wrap short rows (page 132)
and the cuff is cast off using the stretchy
method (page 145).

BOOTIE (MAKE 2)
Using A and Judy's Magic Cast On,
cast on 12 sts. Pm at beg of rnd and
after 6 sts to mark halfway point.
Inc rnd: *K1, kfb, k to 2 sts before m,
kfb, k1; sm, rep from * once (inc 4).
Rep inc rnd once more (20 sts).
Knit 1 rnd.
Rep last 2 rnds 1[2:2:3] times.
24[28:28:32] sts.

SET FOOT PATTERN
Change to B. Knit 1 rnd, inc 1 st in first
half section. 25[29:29:33] sts.
Rnd 1: K1[2:2:2], (k1, p1) to 2[3:3:3] sts
before halfway m, k to end.
Rnd 2: Knit.
Rep last 2 rnds until piece meas
1¾[2½:2¾:3¼]in (4.5[6.5:7.5:8.5]cm),
ending with rnd 1.

SHAPE HEEL
Next rnd: K to halfway m.
Join A but do not break B.
Cont in A only for heel turn.
Short row 1 (RS): K to last st before
halfway m, w&t.

Short row 2 (WS): P to last st, w&t.
Short row 3: K to last st before
wrapped st, w&t.
Short row 4: P to last st before
wrapped st, w&t.
Rep last 2 rows until 4 sts rem
unwrapped, ending with a WS row.
Short row 5 (RS): K to first wrapped st,
k wrap tog with wrapped st, turn.
Short row 6 (WS): P to first wrapped st,
p wrap tog with wrapped st, turn.
Rep last 2 rows until all wrapped sts have
been worked tog with wraps, ending at
halfway m with a WS row.
Break A and cont in B only. K to last st.
Next rnd: K tog last st of last rnd and
first st of next rnd, work patt rnd 1 to
end. 24[28:28:32] sts.

SET CUFF PATTERN
Next rnd: Knit.
Next rnd: (K1, p1) around.
Rep these 2 rnds until rib section meas
1½[2:2¼:2¾]in (4[5:6:7]cm), ending with
a k rnd.
Change to A and cast off using a
stretchy method.

TO FINISH
Weave in ends.

BABY AND TODDLER GIFT SET

Helical stripes are a brilliant way of avoiding jogs when knitting stripes in the round, and are used to add a strong contrast in this cute socks and matching mini bag set, perfect for a new baby and big brother or sister gift.

SIZES

To fit age: 0-6[6-12:12-18]mths
Sock cuff circumference: 3¾[4¼:4¾]in (9.5[10.5:12]cm)
Foot length: 2½[3¼:3¾]in (6.5[8.5:9.5]cm)
Bag width: 3¼in (8cm)
Bag depth: 3¾in (9.5cm)
Handle length: 7in (18cm)
Figures in square brackets refer to larger sizes: where there is only one set of figures this applies to all sizes.

YOU WILL NEED

John Arbon Devonia 4 Ply 50% Exmoor Blueface, 30% Devon Bluefaced Leicester, 20% Devon Wensleydale wool (approx 424yd/388m per 100g)
Small amount in Devonia Cream (A)
Small amount in Cinder Glow (B)
2.5mm and 2.75mm double-pointed or circular needles
Stitch holders
Stitch markers
Tapestry needle

TENSION

30 sts and 39 rnds to 4in (10cm) over st st in the round using 2.75mm needles.
Use larger or smaller needles if necessary to obtain correct tension.

PATTERN NOTES

These socks are worked from the toe up, cast on using Judy's Magic Cast On (page 116). The main pattern is helical stripes (page 136). The heel is turned using shadow-wrap short rows (page 132) and the cuff is cast off using the stretchy method (page 145). The bag is also cast on using Judy's Magic Cast On and the handle is worked in i-cord. The handle ends are grafted at the end (page 142).

SOCK (MAKE 2)

Using 2.75mm needles and A, cast on 12 sts using Judy's Magic Cast On. Knit 1 rnd, working any twisted sts tbl to untwist them. Pm to mark beg of rnd and after 6 sts for halfway point.
Rnd 1: *K1, m1, k to last st before m, m1, k1; sm, rep from * once (inc 4). Rep rnd 1 another 2 times (24 sts).
Rnd 2: Knit.
Rep rnds 1 and 2 another 1[2:3] times. 28[32:36] sts.

SET HELICAL STRIPES

Rnd 1: Join B and knit 1 rnd.
Rnd 2: Using A, k to last 3 sts in B, slip these 3 sts to RH needle.
Rnd 3: Using B, k to last 3 sts in A, slip these 3 sts to RH needle.

Note: You will not be working full rounds in this section.
Rep rnds 2 and 3 until foot meas 1¾[2¼:2½]in (4.5[6:6.5]cm) or ¾[1:1¼]in (2[2.5:3]cm) less than desired foot length, ending after rnd 3.
Drop B but do not break yarn.
Using A, k to end of rnd.

TURN HEEL

Work in A only throughout this section.
Short row 1 (RS): K to last st before halfway m, w&t.
Short row 2 (WS): P to last st, w&t.
Short row 3: K to last st before wrapped st, w&t.
Short row 4: P to last st before wrapped st, w&t.
Rep rows 3 and 4 until 6 sts rem between wrapped sts, ending after short row 4.
Short row 5 (RS): K to first wrapped st, k wrap tog with wrapped st, turn.
Short row 6 (WS): P to first wrapped st, p wrap tog with wrapped st, turn.
Rep rows 5 and 6 until all wrapped sts have been worked.

LEG

Next rnd: K across heel sts, then k to last 3 sts in B, slip these 3 sts to RH needle.
Cont in helical stripes as set for foot until leg meas ¾[1:1¼]in (1.5[2.5:3]cm)

from top of heel, or ¾in (1.5cm) less than desired length, ending after rnd 3. Break B.

Using A, k to end of rnd.

CUFF

Change to 2.5mm needles.

Next rnd: (K1, p1) to end.

Rep last rnd 4 more times.

Cast off using a stretchy cast off.

TO FINISH

Weave in ends and block if required.

BAG

Using 2.75mm needles and B, cast on 48 sts using Judy's Magic Cast On.

Pm to mark beg of rnd and after 24 sts for halfway point.

Knit 1 rnd, working any twisted sts tbl to untwist them.

Knit 4 rnds.

SET HELICAL STRIPES

Rnd 1: Join A and knit 1 rnd.

Rnd 2: Using B, k to last 3 sts in A, slip these 3 sts to RH needle.

Rnd 3: Using A, k to last 3 sts in B, slip these 3 sts to RH needle.

Note: You will not be working full rounds in this section.

Rep rnds 2 and 3 until Bag meas approx 3½in (9cm), ending after rnd 3.

Using A, k to end of rnd, then work 1 more full rnd in A.

Change to 2.5mm needles.

Next rnd: K2, (k1, p1) to last 2 sts before halfway point, k2; sm, rep from * to end.

Rep last rnd 4 more times.

SET HANDLES

Next rnd: K2, cast off to last 2 sts before halfway point, k2, remove marker, k2, leave these 4 sts on a holder, cast off to last 2 sts, k2, remove marker, k2.

Slip rem sts to a dpn.

Now work i-cord as foll, beg with RS facing even though yarn is not at that end of the work: k4, slip sts to other end of needle to work RS again.

Rep last row until handle meas approx 3½in (9cm), then leave sts on holder.

Rep at the other side of the bag.

TO FINISH

Slip both sets of handle sts back to dpns and graft together.

Once all sts are grafted, sew the two edges together to complete i-cord handle. Weave in ends and block.

BABY LYRA AND PAN

Like a pair of socks, Lyra Belacqua and her daemon Pan are never apart in Philip Pullman's *His Dark Materials* novel trilogy – or even when they are babies in his prequel *La Belle Sauvage*. These socks were inspired by them.

SIZES
To fit age: 0-6[6-12:12-18:18-24]mths
Cuff circumference: 4[4¼:4¾:6]in
(10[11:12:15]cm)
Foot length: 2¾[3¼:3½:4]in
(7[8:9:10]cm) (adjustable)
Figures in square brackets refer to larger sizes: where there is only one set of figures this applies to all sizes.

YOU WILL NEED
Rico Superba Alpaca Luxury Sock
62% virgin wool, 23% polyamide, 15% alpaca
(approx 339yd/310m per 100g)
1[1:1:1] x 100g ball in 004 Silver
2.5mm and 3mm double-pointed or circular needles
Stitch markers

TENSION
30 sts and 36 rnds to 4in (10cm) over st st.
38 sts and 36 rnds to 4in (10cm) over patt.
Use larger or smaller needles if necessary to obtain correct tension.

PATTERN NOTE
These socks are knitted from the toe up, cast on using Judy's Magic Cast On (page 116). The heel is turned using shadow-wrap short rows (page 132) and the cuff is cast off using Jeny's Surprisingly Stretchy Bind Off (page 146).

SOCK (MAKE 2)
Using 2.5mm needles and Judy's Magic Cast On, cast on 14[14:18:18] sts. Pm to mark beg of rnd and after 7[7:9:9] sts to mark halfway point. On first rnd work any twisted sts tbl to untwist them.
Inc rnd: *K1, kfb, k to 2 sts before marker, kfb, k1; rep from * once more (inc 4).
Rep inc rnd 3 more times.
30[30:34:34] sts.
Knit 1 rnd.
SIZES 2, 3 AND 4 ONLY
Rep last 2 rnds 1[2:3] more times.
34[42:46] sts.
ALL SIZES – SET CLUSTER RIB
30[34:42:46] sts: 15[17:21:23] sts each for instep and sole.
Rnds 1-3: K2[3:3:2], (p1, k1) 0[0:1:2] times, p1, k1 tbl, p2, (k1 tbl, p1) twice, p1, k1 tbl, p1, (k1, p1) 0[0:1:2] times, k2[3:3:2], sm, k to end.
Rnd 4: K2[3:3:2], (p1, k1) 0[0:1:2] times, p1, k1 tbl, p2, cl3, p2, k1 tbl, p1, (k1, p1) 0[0:1:2] times, k2[3:3:2], sm, k to end.

Rnds 5 and 6: K2[3:3:2], (p1, k1) 0[0:1:2] times, p1, k1 tbl, p2, k3, p2, k1 tbl, p1, (k1, p1) 0[0:1:2] times, k2[3:3:2], sm, k to end.
Rnd 7: As rnd 4.
Rnds 8-10: As rnd 1.
These 10 rnds form patt and are repeated.
SET HEEL TURN
Place heel turn as foll:
Size 1: Work 1 full 10-rnd patt rep, then work heel turn.
Size 2: Work 1 full 10-rnd patt rep, then work rnds 1-4 again, then turn heel.
Size 3: Work 1 full 10-rnd patt rep, then work rnds 1-7 again, then turn heel.
Size 4: Work 2 full 10-rnd patt reps, then turn heel.
Short row 1 (RS): Patt to last st, w&t.
Short row 2 (WS): P to last st before halfway point m, w&t.
Short row 3: K to st before wrapped st, w&t.
Short row 4: P to st before wrapped st, w&t.
Rep short rows 3 and 4 until 7[7:9:9] sts rem between wraps.
Short row 5 (RS): K to first wrapped st, k wrap tog with wrapped st, turn.
Short row 6 (WS): P to first wrapped st, p wrap tog with wrapped st, turn.

Rep short rows 5 and 6 until all wraps
have been worked tog with wrapped sts,
then cont working in the rnd.

LEG

Cont in patt as set by last patt rnd
worked but work instep patt twice
over all sts.

Cont as set until you have worked
2[3:3:4] full patt reps, or until leg meas
½[½:¾:¾]in (1[1:1.5:1.5]cm) less than
desired length.

CUFF

Rib rnd: K0[1:1:0] (p1, k1) to end[last
st:last st:end], p0[1:1:0].

Rep rib rnd until cuff meas ½[½:¾:¾]in
(1[1:1.5:1.5]cm).

Cast off using a stretchy cast off.

TO FINISH

Weave in ends.

CLUSTER RIB PATTERN

SIZES 0-6 & 6-12 MONTHS

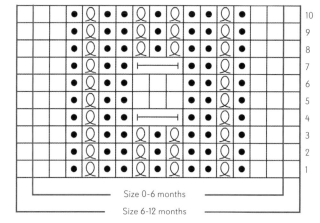

k

p

k1 tbl

cl3

Read all rnds from R to L

SIZES 12-18 MONTHS

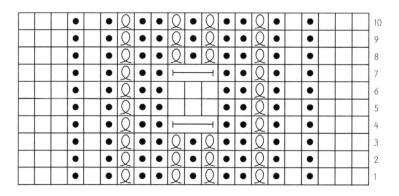

SIZES 18-24 MONTHS

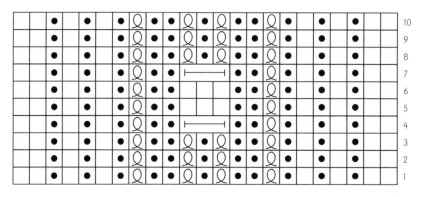

LAVENDER LACE BOOTIES

These pretty lace booties feature a lace pattern inspired by lavender in bloom. Sized from premature up to four years, they make a great gift for a new baby and a brand new big brother or sister.

SIZES
To fit age: Premature[0-3mths: 6-9mths:12-18mths:2yrs:3-4yrs]
Foot length: 3¼[3¾:4¼:5:5¾:6¼]in (8[9.5:11:12.5:14.5:16]cm)
Cuff circumference: ¼[3½:4¼:4¾:5½:6]in (8[9:11:12:14:15.5]cm)
Figures in square brackets refer to larger sizes: where there is only one set of figures this applies to all sizes.

YOU WILL NEED
Cascade 220 Superwash Merino
100% superwash Merino wool (approx 219yd/200m per 100g)
1 x 100g ball in 45 Lavender Heather
4.5mm double-pointed or circular needles
Stitch markers

TENSION
20 sts and 28 rows to 4in (10cm) over st st.
Use larger or smaller needles if necessary to obtain correct tension.

PATTERN NOTES
These booties are knitted from the toe up, cast on using Judy's Magic Cast On (page 116). The heel is turned using shadow-wrap short rows (page 132) and the cuff is cast off using Jeny's Surprisingly Stretchy Bind Off (page 146).

LAVENDER LACE SIZES 1-4
Worked over 11 sts and 6 rnds
Rnd 1: K3, k2tog, yo, k1, yo, ssk, k3.
Rnd 2 and all alt rnds: Knit.
Rnd 3: K2, k2tog, yo, k3, yo, ssk, k2.
Rnd 5: K1, k2tog, yo, k5, yo, ssk, k1.
Rnd 6: Knit.

LAVENDER LACE SIZES 5 AND 6
Worked over 13 sts and 8 rnds
Rnd 1: K4, k2tog, yo, k1, yo, ssk, k4.
Rnd 2 and all alt rnds: Knit.
Rnd 3: K3, k2tog, yo, k3, yo, ssk, k3.
Rnd 5: K2, k2tog, yo, k5, yo, ssk, k2.
Rnd 7: K1, k2tog, yo, k7, yo, ssk, k1.
Rnd 8: Knit.

BOOTIE (MAKE 2)
Cast on 8[8:8:8:12:12] sts using Judy's Magic Cast On. Pm to mark beg of rnd and after 4[4:4:4:6:6] sts to mark halfway point.
Knit 1 rnd, working any twisted sts tbl to untwist them.

SHAPE TOE
Next rnd (inc): *K1, kfb, k to 2 sts before m, kfb, k1, sm; rep from * once more (inc 4). 12[12:12:12:16:16] sts.
Rep last rnd once more.
16[16:16:16:20:20] sts.
Next rnd: Knit.
Next rnd: Rep inc rnd.
20[20:20:20:24:24] sts.
Rep last 2 rnds 0[1:2:3:3:4] more times.
20[24:28:32:36:40] sts.
Next rnd: K5[6:7:8:9:10], kfb, k to end.
21[25:29:33:37:41] sts.

SET FOOT PATTERN
Rnd 1: K0[1:2:3:3:4], working from Chart or written instructions for your size, work rnd 1 of Lavender Lace patt size 1[1:1:1:2:2], k to end.
This rnd sets position of lace patt on instep and st st on sole.
Cont in patt as set until 2 full 6[6:6:6:8:8]-rnd reps have been worked.

TURN HEEL
Short row 1 (RS): K to last st, w&t.
Short row 2 (WS): P to last st before halfway m, w&t.
Short row 3: K to last st before wrapped st, w&t.
Short row 4: P to last st before wrapped st, w&t.

Rep last 2 rows until 4[4:4:4:6:6] sts rem between wrapped sts.

Short row 5 (RS): Sl1, k to first wrapped st, k wrap tog with wrapped st, turn.

Short row 6 (WS): Sl1, p to first wrapped st, p wrap tog with wrapped st, turn.

Rep last 2 rows until all wraps have been worked tog with wrapped sts, ending at beg of rnd after a RS row.

Now return to working in the rnd.

Next rnd: K5[6:7:8:9:10], k2tog, k to end. 20[24:28:32:36:40] sts.

CUFF

Rib rnd 1: (K1, p1) around.

Rib rnd 2: Knit.

Rep these 2 rnds 2[3:3:4:4:5] more times.

Next rnd: Purl.

Next rnd: (K1, p1) around.

Rep last 2 rnds 2[3:3:4:4:5] more times.

Next rnd: Purl.

Cast off pwise using Jeny's Surprisingly Stretchy Bind Off.

TO FINISH

Weave in ends.

LAVENDER LACE SIZES 1-4

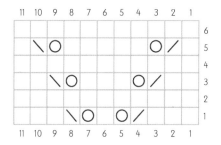

LAVENDER LACE SIZES 5 AND 6

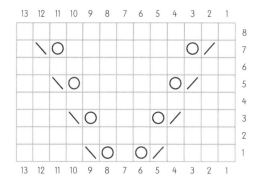

KEY

knit	
O	yo
\	ssk
/	k2tog

CITRUS STRIPE

This cute ear flap hat and bootie combo will style babies and toddlers from top to toe.

SIZE

To fit age: 0-6[6-12:12-18:18-24]mths

Hat brim circumference:
13¾[15¾:18½:20]in (35[40:47:51]cm)

Bootie cuff circumference:
4[4¼:5:6]in (10[11:12.5:15]cm)

Foot length: 2¾[3¼:3¾:4]in
(7[8.5:9.5:10.5]cm)

*Figures in square brackets refer to larger
sizes: where there is only one set of
figures this applies to all sizes.*

YOU WILL NEED

Cascade 220 100% Peruvian Highland
wool (approx 219yd/200m per 100g)
1 x 100g hank in 9615 Bright Nectarine (A)
1 x 100g hank in 7827 Goldenrod (B)
4mm circular or double-pointed needles
Stitch marker
Stitch holders
Tapestry needle
1 small button
Pompom maker (optional)

TENSION

20 sts and 30 rnds to 4in (10cm)
over st st.
*Use larger or smaller needles if
necessary to obtain correct tension.*

PATTERN NOTES

The booties are knitted from the toe
up, cast on using Judy's Magic Cast
On (page 116). The heel is turned using
shadow-wrap short rows (page 132).
Cast off using a stretchy method (page
145). Helical stripes (page 136) are used
to create jogless stripes. The hat ear
pieces are knitted first, then joined to the
main piece as the rest of the brim is cast
on using the knitted method (page 112).

HAT
FIRST EAR PIECE

Using A cast on 4 sts.
Knit 10 rows.
*Row 1 (RS – inc): K2, m1, k2 (5 sts).
Row 2 (inc): K2, m1, k3 (6 sts).
Row 3 (inc): K3, m1, k3 (7 sts).
Row 4: K3, p1, k3.
Row 5 (inc): K3, m1, k to last 3 sts, m1,
k3 (inc 2).
Row 6: K3, p to last 3 sts, k3.
Rep rows 5 and 6 five more times,
ending with a WS row (19 sts).
Next row (RS – inc): K3, k6, kfb,
k to end (20 sts).
Next row: K3, p to last 3 sts, k3.
Next row: Knit.
Cont straight in patt as set by last
2 rows until piece meas 4[4:4¼:4¾]in
(10[10:11:12]cm), ending with a WS row.
Leave sts on a holder.

SECOND EAR PIECE

Using A cast on 4 sts.
Knit 2 rows.
Buttonhole row: K1, k2tog, yo, k1.
Knit 7 more rows.
Work as for First Ear Piece from * to end.

MAIN HAT BODY

Using A and the knitted method,
cast on 5[7:9:10] sts, k across 20 sts of
First Ear Piece, cast on 22[26:34:40] sts,
k across 20 sts of Second Ear Piece,
cast on 5[7:9:10] sts. 72[80:92:100] sts.
Join to work in the round, taking care
not to twist stitches. Pm to mark beg of
rnd at centre of back of head.
Rnd 1: P8[10:12:13], k14, p28[32:40:46],
k14, p to end.
Rnd 2: Knit.
Rep these 2 rnds once more.
Do not break A, join in B.
Knit 1 rnd in B.
SET HELICAL STRIPES
Note: The next rnds will not be full rnds.
Stripe rnd 1: Using A, k to last 3 sts
in B, slip last 3 sts pwise from LH to
RH needle.
Stripe rnd 2: Using B, k to last 3 sts
in A, slip last 3 sts pwise from LH to
RH needle.
Rep last 2 rnds until piece meas
4[4¼:5¼:5½]in (10[11:13:14]cm) from brim,
ending with rnd 2.

Break A and cont in B only. K to end.

Next rnd: Knit, dec 0[2:2:4] sts evenly. 72[78:90:96] sts.

SET CROWN DECREASES

Rnd 1: (K4, k2tog) around. 60[65:75:80] sts.

Rnd 2: Knit.

Rnd 3: (K3, k2tog) around. 48[52:60:64] sts.

Rnd 4: Knit.

Rnd 5: (K2, k2tog) around. 36[39:45:48] sts.

Rnd 6: (K1, k2tog) around. 24[26:30:32] sts.

Rnd 7: (K2tog) around. 12[13:15:16] sts.

Rnd 8: (K2tog) around[to last st:to last st:around], k0[1:1:0]. 6[7:8:8] sts.

Break yarn and use a tapestry needle to thread the end through the rem sts, then pull tight to secure.

TO FINISH

Weave in ends. Make a small pompom and sew on to Hat.

BOOTIE (MAKE 2)

Using A and Judy's Magic Cast On, cast on 12 sts. Pm at beg of rnd and after 6 sts to mark halfway point. On first rnd work any twisted sts tbl to untwist them.

Inc rnd: *Kfb, k to 1 st before m, kfb; sm, rep from * once (inc 4).

Rep inc rnd once more (20 sts).

Knit 1 rnd.

Rep last 2 rnds 1[2:2:3] times. 24[28:28:32] sts.

SET HELICAL STRIPES

Join in B but do not break A.

Knit 1 rnd in B.

Note: The next rnds will not be full rnds.

Next rnd: Using A, k to last 3 sts in B, slip last 3 sts pwise from LH to RH needle.

Next rnd: Using B, k to last 3 sts in A, slip last 3 sts pwise from LH to RH needle.

Rep last 2 rnds until piece meas 1¾[2½:2¾:3¼]in (4.5[6.5:7.5:8.5]cm), ending with A as working yarn.

Do not break B but cont in A only, k to end of rnd.

SHAPE HEEL

Short row 1 (RS): K to last st before halfway m, w&t.

Short row 2 (WS): P to last st, w&t.

Short row 3: K to last st before wrapped st, w&t.

Short row 4: P to last st before wrapped st, w&t.

Rep last 2 rows until 6 sts rem unwrapped, ending with a WS row.

Short row 5 (RS): K to first wrapped st, k wrap tog with wrapped st, turn.

Short row 6 (WS): P to first wrapped st, p wrap tog with wrapped st, turn.

Rep last 2 rows until all wrapped sts have been worked tog with wraps, ending with a WS row.

K to last 3 sts in B, sl3 sts pwise from LH to RH needle.

Break A and cont in B only. K to end.

Next rnd: Knit.

SET RIB

Rib rnd: (K1, p1) around.

Rep rib rnd until rib section meas 2[2¼:2¾:3]in (5[6:7:8]cm).

Cast off using a stretchy method.

TO FINISH

Weave in ends.

BARNEBARN

These footies feature a simple Nordic colourwork motif and are named for the cute Norwegian word for grandchildren. They are sized from toddler to adult and feature a lacy cuff edging as the finishing touch.

SIZES

To fit: Toddler[Child:Adult]
Cuff circumference: 5[7:8¾]in (13[18:23]cm)
Foot length (adjustable): 5[8:10]in (12.5[20:25]cm)
Figures in square brackets refer to larger sizes: where there is only one set of figures this applies to all sizes.

YOU WILL NEED

Scheepjes Downtown 75% wool, 25% nylon
(approx 219yd/200m per 50g)
1 x 50g ball in 401 Sunset (A)
Scheepjes Metropolis 75% wool, 25% nylon
(approx 219yd/200m per 50g)
1 x 50g ball in 053 Santiago (B)
3mm double-pointed or circular needles
3.5mm double-pointed or circular needles (optional – see Pattern Notes)
Stitch markers

TENSION

27 sts and 36 rnds to 4in (10cm) over st st.
Use larger or smaller needles if necessary to obtain correct tension.

PATTERN NOTES

I used larger needles over the colourwork to keep tension even. If your colourwork tends to be tight you may want to do the same thing. Work your tension swatch using one size needle to see whether you need to use a larger size or not. These footies are knitted from the toe up, cast on using Judy's Magic Cast On (page 116). The heel is turned using German Short Rows (page 133) and the cuff is cast off using the stretchy method (page 145).

SOCK (MAKE 2)

Using 3mm needles and A, cast on 8[16:20] sts using Judy's Magic Cast On. Pm to mark beg of rnd and after 4[8:10] sts to mark halfway point. On first rnd work any twisted sts tbl to untwist.

CHART

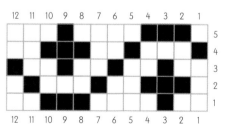

KEY

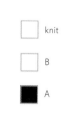

TOE

Next rnd (inc): *K1, m1L, k to last st before m, m1R, k1; rep from * once more (inc 4).
Rep inc rnd 2 more times. 20[28:32] sts.
Knit 1 rnd.
Rep last 2 rnds 2[5:5] more times. 36[48:48] sts.

SIZE 3 ONLY

Rep inc rnd (52 sts).
Knit 2 rnds.
Rep last 3 rows 2 more times (60 sts).

ALL SIZES – FOOT

Knit 1 rnd.
Change to B.
Knit 3 rnds.
Using A and B, work 12-st patt from Chart 3[4:5] times around, working through all 5 rnds of Chart.
Break A and cont in B only in st st until

foot meas 3½[6:7¾]in (8.5[15:19.5]cm)
or 1½[2:2¼]in (4[5:5.5]cm) less than
desired length.

SHAPE HEEL

Using B, k to halfway m. Do not break B.
Join A and work as foll:

Short row 1 (RS): K to last st, w&t.

Short row 2 (WS): Sl1, p to last st, w&t.

Short row 3: K to last st before
wrapped st, w&t.

Short row 4: P to last st before
wrapped st, w&t.

Rep last 2 rows until 4[8:10] sts rem
unwrapped, ending after row 4.

Short row 5 (RS): Sl1, k to first wrapped
st, k wrap tog with wrapped st, turn.

Short row 6 (WS): Sl1, p to first wrapped
st, p wrap tog with wrapped st, turn.

Rep last 2 rows until all wraps have
been worked, ending with row 6 at
halfway m. Break A and k to end in B.

LEG

Cont in B only, work 5[10:15] rnds in st st.
Work from ** to ** as for foot.
Cont in B only, work 5[10:15] rnds in st st.

CUFF

Rib rnd: Using A, work (k1, p1) around.
Rep rib rnd until cuff meas ½[¾:1]in
(1[1.5:2.5]cm).
Change to B.

Next rnd: Knit.

Next rnd: (Yo, k1) around. 72[96:120] sts.
Change to 3.5mm needles.

Next rnd: Knit.
Cast off in A.

TO FINISH

Weave in ends,
Close up any gaps at the heel and block
to measurements, according to yarn
band instructions.

BEST
FOOT
FORWARD

Get stuck into sock
knitting with these
adventurous designs

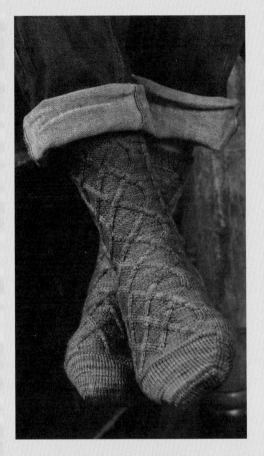

MAJOR TOM'S SOCKS

These are your basic 'vanilla' toe-up socks – but with a heel flap and a gusset for extra shape, perfect for anyone with a high instep.

SIZE
To fit: UK 5-7
Cuff circumference: 6¾in (17cm)
Foot length: 9½in (24cm) (adjustable)

YOU WILL NEED
The Wool Kitchen BFL and Nylon Sock 4 Ply 75% Bluefaced Leicester wool, 25% nylon
(approx 437yd/400m per 100g)
1 x 100g skein in Ground Control (A)
Opal Uni Solid Sock Yarn 75% superwash new wool, 25% polyamide
(approx 465yd/425m per 100g)
Small amount in 2013 Neon Orange (B)
2.5mm double-pointed or
circular needles
Stitch markers

TENSION
32 sts and 44 rnds to 4in (10cm) over st st.
Use larger or smaller needles if necessary to obtain correct tension.

PATTERN NOTES
These socks are knitted from the toe up and cast on using Judy's Magic Cast On (page 116). The heel is turned using German short rows (page 133) and a gusset and heel flap are worked (pages 134 and 129). The cuff is cast off using Jeny's Surprisingly Stretchy Bind Off (page 146).

SOCK (MAKE 2)
Using B and Judy's Magic Cast On, cast on 24 sts. Pm to mark beg of rnd and after 12 sts for halfway point.
SET TOE SHAPING
Rnd 1: Knit, untwisting any twisted sts by knitting them tbl.
Rnd 2 (inc): *K1, kfb, k to 2 sts before halfway m, kfb, k1; sm, rep from * once more (28 sts).
Rnd 3: Rep rnd 2 (32 sts).
Rnd 4: Knit.
Rnd 5 (inc): *K1, m1L, k to last st before halfway m, m1R, k1; sm, rep from * once more (inc 4).
Rnd 6: Knit.
Rep rnds 5 and 6 until you have 60 sts, ending with rnd 6. If using dpns, divide over 4 dpns when it is comfortable to do so.
Knit 1 rnd.
SET FOOT PATT
Change to A and cont in st st in the rnd until Sock meas 5½in (14cm), or 4in (10cm) less than desired foot length.
SET GUSSET
Rnd 1 (inc): K across instep to halfway marker, sm, m1R, pm, k to end of rnd, pm, m1L (62 sts).
Rnd 2: Knit.
Rnd 3 (inc): K across instep sts, sm, m1R, k to end of rnd slipping markers, m1L (inc 2).
Rnd 4: Knit.
Rep rnds 3 and 4 a further 10 times (84 sts).
TURN HEEL
Using A, k to start of sole sts, slipping markers.
Break A and change to B.
Short row 1: K to last sole st, w&t.
Short row 2: P to last st before m, w&t.
Short row 3: K to last st before wrapped st, w&t.
Short row 4: P to last st before wrapped st, w&t.
Rep short rows 3 and 4 a further 7 times until 12 sts remain unwrapped.
SET HEEL FLAP
Row 1 (RS): Working any wrapped sts tog with their wraps as you come to them, k to last sole st, remove marker, ssk (last sole st with first gusset st), pm, turn.
Row 2 (WS): Sl1 wyif, working any wrapped sts tog with their wraps as you come to them, p to last sole st, remove marker, p2tog (last sole st with first gusset st), pm, turn.

Row 3: Sl1 wyib, k to last sole st, remove marker, ssk (last sole st with first gusset st), pm, turn.

Row 4: Sl1 wyif, p to last sole st, remove marker, p2tog (last sole st with first gusset st), pm, turn.

Rep rows 3 and 4 until 1 gusset st remains on each side.

Break B and rejoin A.

With RS facing, sl1 wyib, k to last sole st, remove marker, ssk (last sole st with first gusset st), k to instep sts, k across instep sts, k to last gusset st, k tog last gusset st with first sole st, k to end of sole sts. Start of instep sts now returns to being beg of rnd.

SET LEG
Knit in A until leg meas 3½in (9cm), or 1in (2.5cm) less than desired length.

SET CUFF
Break A, rejoin B.

Knit 1 rnd.

Rib rnd: (K1, p1) around.

Rep rib rnd 7 more times.

Cast off using Jeny's Surprisingly Stretchy Bind Off.

TO FINISH
Weave in ends and block according to yarn band instructions.

JULIET MINI SOCKS

A touch of cashmere and soft Merino wool make these lacy footies with an all-over heart design a wonderful handcrafted present for a beloved friend.

SIZE
To fit: UK 5-7
Foot circumference: 9in (23cm)
Foot length: 10in (25.5cm)

YOU WILL NEED
Gründl Hot Socks Pearl mit Kaschmir
75% superwash Merino wool,
20% polyamide, 5% cashmere
(approx 219yd/200m per 50g)
1 x 50g ball in 16 Powder Pink
2.5mm double-pointed or
circular needles
Stitch markers
Approx 1yd (1m) x 5mm ribbon to trim

TENSION
30 sts and 40 rnds to 4in (10cm)
over st st.
*Use larger or smaller needles if
necessary to obtain correct tension.*

PATTERN NOTES
These footies are knitted from the toe
up, cast on using Judy's Magic Cast
On (page 116). The heel is turned
using shadow-wrap short rows (page
132). A small gusset is added to shape
the instep but it is decreased without
working a heel flap. The socks are cast
off using a standard cast off with a
needle one size larger (page 144),

but you may prefer to use your favourite
stretchy method. If you prefer normal
ankle socks or even longer socks to
mini-socks, simply repeat the 16-row
pattern as many times as you like before
starting the rib. Please note that you
may require more yarn if you do this.

LACY HEARTS PATTERN
Worked over 8 sts and 16 rnds
Rnd 1: Yo, ssk, k6.

CHART   **KEY**

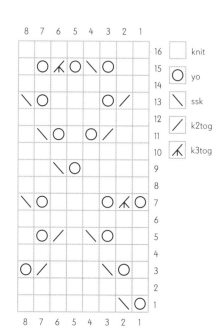

	knit
O	yo
\	ssk
/	k2tog
⋏	k3tog

Rnd 2 and all alt rnds: Knit.
Rnd 3: K1, yo, ssk, k3, k2tog, yo.
Rnd 5: K2, yo, ssk, k1, k2tog, yo, k1.
Rnd 7: Yo, k3tog, yo, k3, yo, ssk.
Rnd 9: K4, yo, ssk, k2.
Rnd 11: K2, k2tog, yo, k1, yo, ssk, k1.
Rnd 13: K1, k2tog, k3, yo, ssk.
Rnd 15: K2, yo, ssk, yo, k3tog, yo, k1.
Rnd 16: Knit.

SOCK (MAKE 2)
Cast on 24 sts using Judy's Magic
Cast On. Pm to mark beg of rnd and
after 12 sts for halfway point.
Set-up rnd: Knit, working any twisted
sts tbl to untwist them.
Inc rnd: (Kfb, k to 1 st before m, kfb)
twice (inc 4).
Rep inc rnd every rnd until you have
72 sts.
SET LACY HEARTS PATTERN
Rnd 1: K2, working from Chart or written
instructions work rnd 1 of Lacy Hearts
Patt 4 times, sm, k to end.
Rnd 2: Knit.
These 2 rnds set Lacy Hearts Patt over
instep and st st over sole. Cont as set
until you have worked 3 full reps of Lacy
Hearts Patt, then work rnds 1-9 again.
SHAPE GUSSET
Next rnd (inc): Patt to m (Lacy Hearts
Patt rnd 10), sm, k1, kfb, k to last 2 sts,

kfb, k1 (inc 2).

Next rnd: Patt to m, sm, k to end.
These 2 rnds set gusset inc patt.
Rep inc rnd on every alt rnd until you
have worked rnd 15 of patt (78 sts).

TURN HEEL

Short row 1 (RS): Patt to m (Lacy Hearts
Patt rnd 16), sm, k1, kfb, k to last 2 sts, kfb,
w&t (80 sts).

Short row 2 (WS): P to halfway m, w&t.

Short row 3: K to st before wrapped
st, w&t.

Short row 4: P to st before wrapped
st, w&t.

Rep rows 3 and 4 until 12 sts rem
unwrapped.

Short row 5 (RS): K to first wrapped st,
k wrap tog with wrapped st, turn.

Short row 6 (WS): P to first wrapped st,
p wrap tog with wrapped st, turn.

Rep rows 5 and 6 until all wrapped sts
have been worked, then k to end of rnd.

SET ANKLE PATT

Next rnd (dec): K2tog, work rnd 1 of
Lacy Hearts Patt 4 times, k2tog, sm,
*(k2tog, k8) twice, k2tog; rep from *
once more (72 sts).

Next rnd: Knit.

Next rnd: Work rnd 3 of Lacy Hearts
Patt 9 times around.
This rnd sets position of Lacy Hearts
Patt. Cont as set until you have
completed rnd 16 of patt or to desired
length (see Pattern Notes).

Next rnd (dec): *P2tog, (p1, k1) twice,
(p2, k1, p1, k1) 5 times; rep from * to end
(70 sts).

Rib rnd 1: (P2, k3) around.

Rib rnd 2: (P2, k1, p1, k1) around.
Rep rnds 1 and 2 a further 3 times,
then rnd 1 again.
Cast off in rib.

TO FINISH

Weave in ends. Block to open lace.
Using a large-eyed tapestry needle
thread ribbon through top row of
Lacy Hearts Patt. Sew ends together
or tie in a bow.

ALOE THERE

The wool in these socks is infused with aloe vera to soothe tired, sore feet and a simple ribbed cable adds a touch of style.

SIZE

To fit: Average adult woman[man]
UK 5-8[9-12]
Cuff circumference: 7½[8¼]in
(19[21]cm)
Foot length: 8¾[10¼]in (22[26]cm)
(adjustable)
Figures in square brackets refer to larger sizes: where there is only one set of figures this applies to all sizes.

YOU WILL NEED

Hjertegarn Aloe Sockwool 75% wool,
25% polyamide
(approx 459yd/420m per 100g)
1[1] x 100g ball in 434 Light Grey
2.5mm double-pointed or
circular needles
Cable needle
Stitch markers
Blunt-ended tapestry needle

TENSION

34 sts and 46 rnds to 4in (10cm)
over st st.
Cable Rib Patt meas 1¾ x 1½in
(4.5 x 4cm).
Use larger or smaller needles if necessary to obtain correct tension.

PATTERN NOTES

These socks are worked from the top down, cast on using the long-tail method (page 113) and joined using a jogless join (page 115). A slip stitch pattern is worked over the heel flap, then the heel is turned and a gusset is worked (page 130). At the end the toe stitches are grafted together (page 142).

TIP

If you don't have a cable needle small enough to work the cables in this design, arrange your stitches over dpns so that the first 12 sts of the Cable Rib Patt fall at the end of one dpn and the next 12 fall at the start of another. When you have worked up to the start of the cabling, the 8 sts you need to slip to a cable needle will be the last 8 sts on your dpn, so you can simply hold this at the back and work the following 8 sts from the next needle. You may then need to slip the 8 sts from the held dpn on to the LH needle to work them.

CABLE RIB PATTERN

Worked over 24 sts and 21 rnds
Rnd 1: P4, (p1, k1) 8 times, p4.
Rep rnd 1 another 9 times.

Rnd 11 (cable): P4, C16B, p4.
Rep row 1 another 10 times.

CABLE RIB TWIST PATTERN

Worked over 24 sts and 20 rnds
Rnd 1: P4, (p1, k1) 8 times, p4.
Rnd 2: As rnd 1.
Rnd 3: P5, (k1, p1) 3 times, TW3,
(p1, k1) 3 times, p4.
Rnd 4: As rnd 1.
Rep rnds 3 and 4 another 7 times.
Rep rnd 1 twice more.

SOCK (MAKE 2)

Cast on 72[80] sts. Join to work in the round, taking care not to twist sts, and pm to mark beg of rnd and after 36[40] sts for halfway point.

CUFF

Rib rnd: (K1, p1) to end.
Rep rib rnd until piece meas approx 1in (2.5cm).

SET MAIN PATTERN

Rnd 1: K6[8], using Chart or written instructions work rnd 1 of Cable Rib Patt, k6[8], sm, k to end.
This rnd sets position of Cable Rib Patt and st st. Cont in patt as set until you have worked 21-rnd Cable Rib Patt a total of 2[3] times, ending after row 21.

HEEL FLAP

Turn and cont on second half of sts only for heel flap, as foll:

Note: Slip all stitches pwise.

Set-up row (WS): Sl1, p to halfway m, turn.

Row 1 (RS): (Sl1, k1) to end.

Row 2: Sl1, p to end.

Row 3: Sl2, (k1, sl1) to last 2 sts, k2.

Row 4: As row 2.

These 4 rows set heel flap patt. Rep rows 1-4 another 12[13] times, then row 1 once more. Heel flap meas approx 2¾in (7cm).

HEEL TURN

Short row 1 (WS): Sl1, p18[20], p2tog, p1, turn.

Short row 2 (RS): Sl1, k3, ssk, k1, turn.

Short row 3: Sl1, p to 1 st before gap, p2tog, p1, turn.

Short row 4: Sl1, k to 1 st before gap, ssk, k1, turn.

Rep last 2 rows until all sts of heel flap have been worked. 20[22] sts rem for sole. Pm at end of heel flap to mark temporary new beg of rnd.

GUSSET AND FOOT

Set-up rnd 1: Pick up and k26[28] sts up side of heel flap, sm, pick up 1 st between side sts and instep sts, patt across 36[40] instep sts working Cable Rib Patt as set, pick up and k1 st between instep sts and side sts, slip halfway point marker, pick up and k26[28] sts down side of heel flap, k across 20[22] sole sts. 110[120] sts.

Set-up rnd 2: K tbl to last 3 sts before m, k2tog, k1 tbl, sm, k2tog, patt to 2 sts before m, ssk, sm, k1 tbl, ssk, k23[25] tbl, k to end.

Rnd 1: K to m, sm, patt to m, sm, k to end.

Rnd 2 (dec): K to 3 sts before m, k2tog, k1, sm, patt to m, sm, k1, ssk, k to end (dec 2).

Rep rnds 1 and 2 until 72[80] sts rem: 36[40] in patt for instep and 36[40] in st st for sole. Remove temporary beg of rnd marker.

The marker at start of instep now marks beg of rnd again.

Cont in patt as set until you have worked Cable Rib Patt a total of 3[5] times, then rnds 1-11 again. Beg with rnd 1, work Cable Rib Twist Patt once in place of Cable Rib Patt. Beg with rnd 11, return to working in Cable Rib Patt as set. Rep rnd 1 of Cable Rib Patt 10 more times.

Tip: Adjust foot length here by working last rnd fewer or more times.

CABLE RIB PATTERN

24	23	22	21	20	19	18	17	16	15	14	13	12	11	10	9	8	7	6	5	4	3	2	1	
•	•	•	•		•		•		•		•		•		•		•		•	•	•	•	•	21
•	•	•	•		•		•		•		•		•		•		•		•	•	•	•	•	20
•	•	•	•		•		•		•		•		•		•		•		•	•	•	•	•	19
•	•	•	•		•		•		•		•		•		•		•		•	•	•	•	•	18
•	•	•	•		•		•		•		•		•		•		•		•	•	•	•	•	17
•	•	•	•		•		•		•		•		•		•		•		•	•	•	•	•	16
•	•	•	•		•		•		•		•		•		•		•		•	•	•	•	•	15
•	•	•	•		•		•		•		•		•		•		•		•	•	•	•	•	14
•	•	•	•		•		•		•		•		•		•		•		•	•	•	•	•	13
•	•	•	•		•		•		•		•		•		•		•		•	•	•	•	•	12
•	•	•	•	C16B cable cross															•	•	•	•	•	11
•	•	•	•		•		•		•		•		•		•		•		•	•	•	•	•	10
•	•	•	•		•		•		•		•		•		•		•		•	•	•	•	•	9
•	•	•	•		•		•		•		•		•		•		•		•	•	•	•	•	8
•	•	•	•		•		•		•		•		•		•		•		•	•	•	•	•	7
•	•	•	•		•		•		•		•		•		•		•		•	•	•	•	•	6
•	•	•	•		•		•		•		•		•		•		•		•	•	•	•	•	5
•	•	•	•		•		•		•		•		•		•		•		•	•	•	•	•	4
•	•	•	•		•		•		•		•		•		•		•		•	•	•	•	•	3
•	•	•	•		•		•		•		•		•		•		•		•	•	•	•	•	2
•	•	•	•		•		•		•		•		•		•		•		•	•	•	•	•	1
24	23	22	21	20	19	18	17	16	15	14	13	12	11	10	9	8	7	6	5	4	3	2	1	

KEY

☐ knit

● purl

⟋⟍ C16B

Foot meas approx 6¾[8¼]in (17[21]cm) or 2in (5cm) less than desired length.

SHAPE TOE

Knit 1 rnd.

Next rnd (dec): *K1, ssk, k to 3 sts before m, k2tog, k1; sm, rep from * to end (dec 4).

Knit 1 rnd.

Rep last 2 rnds 5 more times.

Now rep dec rnd only until 24 sts rem. Graft toe sts tog.

TO FINISH

Weave in ends.

Block gently.

CABLE RIB TWIST PATTERN

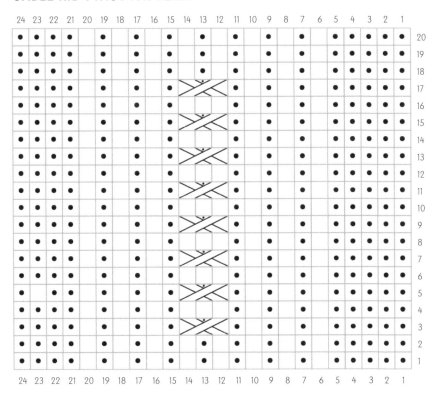

KEY

☐ knit

● purl

⟩⟨ TW3

MOLTON

These simple stripy socks are perfect for sock knitting newbies and are named after the John Arbon mill in Devon, which spins its Exmoor Sock Yarn from the fleece of local sheep.

SIZE

To fit: Average adult – foot length is easily adjustable.
Circumference: 8in (20cm)
Foot length: 10¼in (26cm) (adjustable)

YOU WILL NEED

John Arbon Exmoor Sock 4 Ply
60% Exmoor Blueface, 20% Corriedale, 10% Zwartbles wool, 10% nylon
1 x 50g ball in Bell Heather (A)
1 x 50g ball in Mackerel-Sky (B)
1 x 50g ball in Whortleberries (C)
Scrap yarn in a contrast colour
2.5mm double-pointed or circular needles
Stitch markers
Blunt-ended tapestry needle

TENSION

30 sts and 45 rnds to 4in (10cm) over st st stripe patt.
Use larger or smaller needles if necessary to obtain correct tension.

TIP

Always stop at beg of rnd marker to avoid losing track of which yarn you're working with.

PATTERN NOTES

These socks are knitted from the toe up, cast on using Judy's Magic Cast On (page 116). The main pattern is in helical stripes (page 136) and the heel is an afterthought heel (page 126). The cuff is cast off using a stretchy method (page 145). The afterthought heel is worked last and the stitches grafted together (page 142).

SOCK (MAKE 2)

Using A and Judy's Magic Cast On, cast on 24 sts. Pm to mark beg of rnd and after 12 sts for halfway point.
Set-up rnd: Knit 1 rnd, working any twisted sts tbl to untwist them.

SET TOE INCREASES

Rnd 1: *K1, m1L, k to 1 st before m, m1R, k1; rep from * once (inc 4).
Rnd 2: Knit.
Rep rnds 1 and 2 until you have 60 sts, ending with rnd 2.
Break A.

SET HELICAL STRIPES

Note: Do not break B or C during entire stripe section. Please note that you will not be working in full rounds in this section.

Rnd 1: Knit in B.
Rnd 2: Using C, k to last 3 sts, slip these 3 sts pwise to RH needle.
Rnd 3: Using B, k to last 3 sts in C. Slip these 3 sts pwise to RH needle.
Rnd 4: Using C, k to last 3 sts in B. Slip these 3 sts pwise to RH needle.
Rep rnds 3 and 4 for helical stripe patt.
Cont as set until piece meas approx 8in (20cm) or 2in (5cm) less than desired foot length.

POSITION AFTERTHOUGHT HEEL

Take a note of where your stripe colour change is. If it is in the first half of the stitches, you will position your heel across the second half; if it is in the second half your heel will be positioned across the first half of the stitches. If the colour change is in between the two halves you may wish to work a couple of extra rounds (or unknit a few rounds) until it sits neatly in one half or the other.

WHERE COLOUR CHANGE IS IN THE FIRST HALF OF STITCHES

Next rnd: Patt to m, work across rem 30 sts in contrast yarn, then slip the 30 sts just worked back to LH needle and work them again in patt.

WHERE COLOUR CHANGE IS IN THE SECOND HALF OF STITCHES

Next rnd: Work across first 30 sts in contrast yarn, slip these 30 sts just worked back to LH needle and work them again in patt.

ALL SOCKS

Cont in patt as set until piece meas approx 12in (30cm) or 1in (2.5cm) less than desired leg length, measured from contrast yarn.

SET CUFF

Break B and C and join A.

Next rnd: Using A, (k1, p1) around.

Rep last rnd for 1in (2.5cm).

Cast off using a stretchy cast off.

AFTERTHOUGHT HEEL

Pick up sts on either side of scrap yarn (60 sts).

Set-up rnd: Using A, pm to mark beg of rnd, pick up and k1 in between 2 sets of sts, k across first 30 sts, pm to mark halfway point, pick up and k1 in between 2 sets of sts, k to end (62 sts).

Knit 1 rnd.

SET HEEL DECREASES

Dec rnd 1: *(Ssk) twice, k to 3 sts before m, k2tog, k1; sm, rep from * once more (56 sts).

Knit 3 rnds.

**Dec rnd 2: *K1, ssk, k to 3 sts before m, k2tog, k1; sm, rep from * once (dec 4).

Knit 2 rnds.

Rep from ** once more, then work dec rnd 2 every alt rnd until you have 24 sts. Graft heel stitches together.

TO FINISH

Weave in ends. Block.

LYRA AND PAN

Super-soft alpaca adds a gentle touch and a slight haze to this comfortable sock yarn, worked with a Japanese-style cluster stitch pattern and inspired by Lyra and her daemon Pan, from Philip Pullman's *His Dark Materials* novels.

SIZES
S[M:L:XL]
To fit: UK 3-5[6-8:9-10:11-12]
Ankle circumference: 5½[6¼:7:8]in (14[16:18:20]cm)
Foot length: 8[8¾:9½:10¼]in (20[22:24:26]cm)
Size note: The socks are calculated with negative ease for both ankle circumference and foot length and are stretchy.
Figures in square brackets refer to larger sizes: where there is only one set of figures this refers to all sizes.

YOU WILL NEED
Rico Superba Alpaca Luxury Sock
62% wool, 23% polyamide, 15% alpaca (approx 339yd/310m per 100g)
One-colour version:
1[1:1:1] x 100g ball in 006 Black
Two-colour version:
1[1:1:1] x 100g ball in 004 Silver (A)
1[1:1:1] x 100g ball in 005 Grey (B)
2.5mm and 3mm double-pointed or circular needles
Stitch markers
Blunt-ended tapestry needle

TENSION
30 sts and 36 rnds to 4in (10cm) over st st.
38 sts and 36 rnds to 4in (10cm) over patt.
Each 28-rnd patt rep meas 3¼in (8.5cm)
Use larger or smaller needles if necessary to obtain correct tension.

TIPS
I knitted this pattern using a set of 5 dpns, which worked out well as the pattern can easily be divided into 4 sections.
To adjust foot length, take the length of the foot you want to fit and subtract ¾in (2cm), then subtract the length of the toe for the size you are making (see toe decrease section). Each 28-rnd patt rep meas 3¼in (8.5cm). Calculate how many full repeats you want to work and then end on rnd 5 or rnd 9. If this doesn't take you to the correct length, rep rnd 1 until you are ready to work the toe.

PATTERN NOTES
One-colour version is photographed in size 2 (M), two-colour version in size 3 (L). These socks are knitted from the top down, cast on using the long-tail method (page 113) and joined with a jogless join (page 115). A heel flap and gusset are worked, with the heel in a slip stitch pattern (pages 130 and 129). The toe stitches are grafted together to finish (page 142).

CLUSTER STITCH
Worked over 24[28:32:36] sts and 28 rnds
Rnds 1-5: *(P1, k1) 3[4:5:6] times, p2, (k1 tbl, p1) twice, (p1, k1 tbl) twice, p2, (k1, p1) 3[4:5:6] times.
Rnd 6: *(P1, k1) 3[4:5:6] times, (p2, cl3) twice, p2, (k1, p1) 3[4:5:6] times.
Rnds 7-9: *(P1, k1) 3[4:5:6] times, (p2, k3) twice, p2, (k1, p1) 3[4:5:6] times.
Rnd 10: As rnd 6.
Rnds 11-15: As rnd 1.
**Rnd 16: As rnd 6.
Rnds 17-19: As rnd 7.**
Rnds 20-27: Rep from ** to ** 2 more times.
Rnd 28: As rnd 6.
These 28 rnds form patt.

ONE-COLOUR VERSION (MAKE 2)
CUFF
Using 2.5mm needles cast on 48[56:64:72] sts.

Join to work in the round, taking care
not to twist sts, and pm to mark beg
of rnd and after 24[28:32:36] sts for
halfway point.
Knit 1 rnd.

SET RIB

Rnd 1: *(P1, k1) 3[4:5:6] times, p2, (k1 tbl,
p1) twice, (p1, k1 tbl) twice, p2, (k1, p1)
3[4:5:6] times; rep from * once.
Rep last rnd 7 more times.

SET CLUSTER STITCH PATTERN

Change to 3mm needles.
Using Chart or written instructions, work
Cluster Stitch patt twice across each rnd.
Cont in patt as set until row 24 has
been completed, then cont and end
after rnd 5.

HEEL FLAP

Rnd 1: K to m***, turn and work on
these 24[28:32:36] sts only for heel flap.
Row 1 (WS): (Sl1, p1) to end, turn.
Row 2: Sl1, k to end.
Rep these 2 rows 15 more times, ending
after a row 2. Heel flap meas approx
2½in (6.5cm).

TURN HEEL

Short row 1 (WS): Sl1, p12[14:16:18],
p2tog, p1, turn.
Short row 2: Sl1, k3, ssk, k1, turn.
Short row 3: Sl1, p4 (to last st before
gap), p2tog, p1, turn.
Short row 4: Sl1, k5 (to last st before
gap), ssk, k1, turn.
Cont as set by rows 3 and 4 until no sts
rem after gap, ending after a RS row.
The last 2 rows will not have a k1 or p1
after the ssk or p2tog. 12[14:16:18] sts.

CLUSTER STITCH PATTERN

KEY

k		Size S: rep 24 sts twice per rnd	
• p		Size M: rep 28 sts twice per rnd	
Q k1 tbl		Size L: rep 32 sts twice per rnd	
⊢——⊣ cl3		Size XL: rep 36 sts twice per rnd	

REJOIN IN THE ROUND

After last row of heel, cont on RS as foll:
Pm (temporary beg of rnd marker),
pick up and k1 st in each of 16 slipped sts
up side of heel flap and 1 st in between
heel flap and sts for top of foot****, sm
(original halfway marker), work across
instep as foll: k2, (p1, k1) 2[3:4:5] times,
(p2, cl3) twice, p2, (k1, p1) 2[3:4:5] times
(patt row 6) to last 2 sts before m, k2,
sm, pick up and k1 st between top of
foot and heel flap and 16 sts down side
of heel flap, k across 12[14:16:18] heel sts.
70[76:82:88] sts.

Set-up rnd (dec): K13 tbl, (k2tog) twice,
sm, patt to next m, sm, (ssk) twice, k13
tbl, k to end. 68[74:80:86] sts.

Rnd 1: K to first instep marker, sm, patt
to next m, sm, k to end.

Rnd 2 (dec): K to 2 sts before first
instep marker, k2tog, sm, patt to next m,
sm, ssk, k to end (dec 2).

Rep last 2 rnds until 48[56:64:72] sts
rem: 24[28:32:36] in patt for instep
(original pattern but with 2 sts in st st
at each side) and 24[28:32:36] in st st
across sole. Remove temporary beg of
rnd marker. First instep marker (original
halfway point) now becomes beg of
rnd marker. Leave the second instep
marker in place to mark halfway point.

FOOT

Cont straight as now set until sole
meas approx 5¾[6½:6¾:7½]in
(14.5[16.5:17.5:19]cm) from tip of heel or
2¼[2¼:2½:2¾]in (5.5[5.5:6.5:7]cm) less
than desired length, ending after rnd
5 or 9 (see Tips).

SET TOE DECREASES

Knit 1 rnd.

Toe dec rnd: *K1, ssk, k to 3 sts before m,
k2tog, k1, sm; rep from * to end (dec 2).

Knit 2 rnds.
Rep the last 3 rnds 1[1:2:3] more times,
then work toe dec rnd every alt rnd until
20 sts rem.
Graft sts together.

TO FINISH

Weave in ends.
Block if required.

TWO-COLOUR VERSION

Using B, cast on as for One-colour
Version and work as set to 'Set cluster rib'.
Change to A and work as set for One-
colour Version to *** (just after start of
heel flap).
Change to B and work as set for One-
colour Version to **** (shortly after start
of 'Rejoin in the round' section).
Change to A and work as set for One-
colour Version to 'Set toe decreases'.
Change to B and work as set to end.

SUNSHINE SOCKS

Put a bit of sunshine in your step with these socks featuring a textured design inspired by the sunrise, and knitted in a glorious hand-dyed yarn.

SIZE
To fit: UK 5-7
Cuff circumference: 7in (18cm)
Foot length (adjustable): 9¾in (25cm)

YOU WILL NEED
The Wool Barn Cashmere Sock 4 Ply
80% superwash extrafine Merino wool, 10% cashmere, 10% nylon
(approx 383yd/350m per 100g)
1 x 100g hank in Honey Bee
2.5mm double-pointed or circular needles
Stitch markers

TENSION
29 sts and 44 rnds to 4in (10cm) over st st, after blocking.
Each 12-rnd Sunshine Lace rep meas 1¼in (3cm) long.
Use larger or smaller needles if necessary to obtain correct tension.

PATTERN NOTES
These socks can knitted from the toe up or the top down. For the toe-up version, cast on using Judy's Magic Cast On (page 116) and cast off using Jeny's Surprisingly Stretchy Bind Off (page 146). The top-down version is cast on using the long-tail method (page 113) and joined in the round with a jogless join (page 115). The toe stitches are grafted at the end (page 142). In both versions the heel is turned using shadow-wrap short rows (page 132). To alter foot or leg length, work more or fewer rows of patt before working heel turn, until foot meas approx 2in (5cm) less than finished length and leg meas approx 1in (2.5cm) less than finished length. You do not need to turn the heel at a particular point of Sunshine Lace patt, but leg and toe should end at the end of a Sunshine Lace patt rep.

SUNSHINE LACE TOE UP
Worked over 27 sts and 12 rnds
Rnds 1 and 2: K1, p1, k1 tbl, p1, k19, p1, k1 tbl, p1, k1.
Rnd 3: K1, p1, k1 tbl, p1, (ssk, yo) twice, (k1, p1) 5 times, k1, (yo, k2tog) twice, p1, k1 tbl, p1, k1.
Rnd 4: K1, p1, k1 tbl, p1, k4, (p1, k1) 5 times, p1, k4, p1, k1 tbl, p1, k1.
Rnd 5: K1, p1, k1 tbl, p1, k1, (ssk, yo) twice, (p1, k1) 4 times, p1, (yo, k2tog) twice, k1, p1, k1 tbl, p1, k1.
Rnd 6: K1, p1, k1 tbl, p1, k6, (p1, k1) 3 times, p1, k6, p1, k1 tbl, p1, k1.
Rnd 7: K1, p1, k1 tbl, p1, k2, (ssk, yo) twice, (k1, p1) 3 times, k1, (yo, k2tog) twice, k2, p1, k1 tbl, p1, k1.
Rnd 8: Rep rnd 6.
Rnd 9: K1, p1, k1 tbl, p1, k3, (ssk, yo) twice, (p1, k1) twice, p1, (yo, k2tog) twice, k3, p1, k1 tbl, p1, k1.
Rnd 10: K1, p1, k1 tbl, p1, k8, p1, k1, p1, k8, p1, k1 tbl, p1, k1.
Rnd 11: K1, p1, k1 tbl, p1, k4, (ssk, yo) twice, k1, (yo, k2tog) 3 times, k4, p1, k1 tbl, p1, k1.
Rnd 12: Rep rnd 1.

SUNSHINE LACE TOP DOWN
Worked over 27 sts and 12 rnds
Rnd 1: K1, p1, k1 tbl, p1, k19, p1, k1 tbl, p1, k1.
Rnd 2: K1, p1, k1 tbl, p1, k4, (k2tog, yo) twice, k1, (yo, ssk) 3 times, k4, p1, k1 tbl, p1, k1.
Rnd 3: K1, p1, k1 tbl, p1, k8, p1, k1, p1, k8, p1, k1 tbl, p1, k1.
Rnd 4: K1, p1, k1 tbl, p1, k3, (k2tog, yo) twice, (p1, k1) twice, p1, (yo, ssk) twice, k3, p1, k1 tbl, p1, k1.
Rnd 5: K1, p1, k1 tbl, p1, k6, (p1, k1) 3 times, p1, k6, p1, k1 tbl, p1, k1.
Rnd 6: K1, p1, k1 tbl, p1, k2, (k2tog, yo) twice, (k1, p1) 3 times, k1, (yo, ssk) twice, k2, p1, k1 tbl, p1, k1.
Rnd 7: Rep rnd 5.

Rnd 8: K1, p1, k1 tbl, p1, k1, (k2tog, yo) twice, (p1, k1) 4 times, p1, (yo, ssk) twice, k1, p1, k1 tbl, p1, k1.

Rnd 9: K1, p1, k1 tbl, p1, k4, (p1, k1) 5 times, p1, k4, p1, k1 tbl, p1, k1.

Rnd 10: K1, p1, k1 tbl, p1, (k2tog, yo) twice, (k1, p1) 5 times, k1, (yo, ssk) twice, p1, k1 tbl, p1, k1.

Rnds 11 and 12: Rep rnd 1.

TOE-UP SOCK (MAKE 2)

Cast on 24 sts using Judy's Magic Cast On. Pm to mark beg of rnd and after 12 sts for halfway point.

Knit 1 rnd, working any twisted sts tbl to untwist them.

Inc rnd 1: *Sm, k1, m1L, k to 1 st before m, m1R, k1; rep from * once more (28 sts).

Inc rnd 2: *Sm, k1, yo, k to 1 st before m, yo, k1; rep from * once more (32 sts).

Inc rnd 3: Rep inc rnd 1, working yarn overs from previous rnd tbl to avoid holes (36 sts).

Inc rnd 4: Rep inc rnd 2 (40 sts).

Next rnd: Knit.

Inc rnd: Rep inc rnd 1 (44 sts).

Rep last 2 rnds 3 more times (56 sts – 28 each for instep and sole).

Knit 2 rnds.

Inc rnd: K13, k2tog, k to m, sm, k1, m1L, k to last st, m1R, k1 (57 sts: 27 for instep and 30 for sole).

Knit 3 rnds.

SET FOOT PATT

Working from Toe-Up Chart or written instructions, work Toe-Up Sunshine Lace patt as foll:

Rnd 1: Work Sunshine Lace Toe-Up patt to m, sm, k to end.

Rnd 1 sets foot patt.

Cont in patt as set until you have worked 6 reps of Sunshine Lace patt, ending after rnd 11 of the last of those patt reps. Foot meas approx 8in (20cm).

TURN HEEL

***Short row 1 (RS): Patt across instep sts as set, sm, k to last st, w&t.

Short row 2 (WS): P to last st before halfway m, w&t.

Short row 3: K to 1 st before wrapped st, w&t.

Short row 4: P to 1 st before wrapped st, w&t.

Rep short rows 3 and 4 until 12 sts rem between wrapped sts.

Short row 5 (RS): Sl1, k to first wrapped

SUNSHINE LACE TOE UP

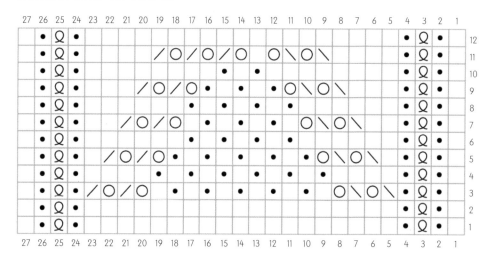

SUNSHINE LACE TOP DOWN

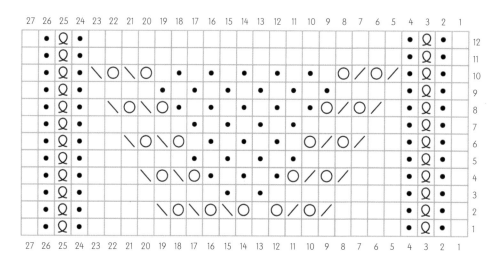

KEY

	knit
Ω	purl
•	k1 tbl
\	k2tog
/	ssk
O	yo

st, k wrap tog with wrapped st, turn.

Short row 6 (WS): Sl1, p to first wrapped st, p wrap tog with wrapped st, turn.***

Rep last 2 rows until all wraps have been worked tog with wrapped sts, then k to end of rnd, dec 1 st at centre of heel sts (56 sts: 27 for instep and 29 for sole). Now return to working in the round.

SET LEG PATT

Rnd 1: Work Sunshine Lace patt to m, sm, (p1, k1 tbl) to last st, p1.

Note: You may want to work first and last st of Sunshine Lace patt as k1 tbl from this point, to fit into rib patt.

Rnd 1 sets leg patt.

Cont in patt as set until you have worked a total of 4 reps of Sunshine Lace patt, ending after rnd 12. Leg meas approx 4in (10cm).

SET CUFF

**Rib rnd: (K1 tbl, p1) around.

Rep rib rnd until cuff meas 1in (2.5cm).**

Cast off using Jeny's Surprisingly Stretchy Bind Off.

TOP-DOWN SOCK (MAKE 2)

Cast on 56 sts using the long-tail method. Join to work in the round, taking care not to twist sts. Pm to mark beg of rnd and after 27 sts for halfway point

You have 27 sts for front of leg and 29 sts for back of leg.

Work cuff as for Toe-Up Socks, working from ** to **.

SET SUNSHINE LACE

Working from Top-Down Chart or written instructions, work Top-Down Sunshine Lace patt across 27 sts, sm, (p1, k1 tbl) to last st, p1.

Note: You may wish to work first and last sts of Sunshine Lace patt as k1 tbl,

to fit in with the rest of the rib patt, up to heel turn.

This rnd sets position of Sunshine Lace patt over front of leg and twisted rib over back of leg. Cont in patt as set until you have worked 4 full reps of patt, ending after rnd 11. On next rnd, inc 1 st at centre of back of leg. Leg meas approx 5in (12.5cm). (57 sts: 27 for instep and 30 for heel).

TURN HEEL

Work as for Toe-Up Socks from *** to ***.

Rep last 2 rows until all wraps have been worked together with wrapped sts, then k to end of rnd.

SET FOOT PATT

Rnd 1: Work Sunshine Lace patt as set to m, sm, k to end.

Rnd 1 sets foot patt.

Cont in patt as set until you have worked 6 full reps of Sunshine Lace patt,

or to approx 5cm (2in) less than desired foot length, ending after rnd 12 of patt. Foot meas approx 8in (20cm).

SHAPE TOE

Knit 3 rnds, inc 1 st at centre of instep on last rnd so you have 58 sts: 28 on instep and 30 on sole.

Dec rnd: K to m, sm, k1, ssk, k to last 3 sts, k2tog, k1. (56 sts: 28 each on instep and sole).

Knit 2 rnds.

Dec rnd: *K1, ssk, k to last 3 sts, k2tog, k1; sm, rep from * once more (dec 4).

Next rnd: Knit.

Rep last 2 rnds 3 more times (44 sts), then work dec rnd every rnd until 24 sts rem.

Graft toe sts tog.

TO FINISH

Weave in ends. Block to measurements, according to yarn band instructions.

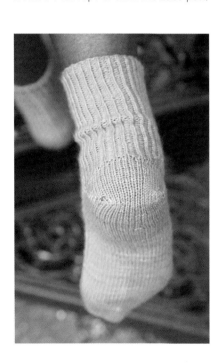

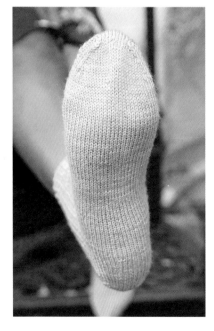

TWISTY SHEEP

Pure British wool can be tough enough for sock knitting, even without nylon.
This undyed blend offers a deliciously crunchy knit in a glorious natural shade.

SIZE
To fit: Adult man UK 9-11
Leg circumference: 8in (20cm)
Leg length: 4¾in (12cm)
Foot length: 11in (28cm)

YOU WILL NEED
Daughter of a Shepherd Brume 4 Ply
50% Hebridean, 25% Zwartbles,
25% Exmoor Blueface pure undyed wool
(approx 437yd/400m per 100g)
1 x 100g hank
2.75mm double-pointed or
circular needles
Stitch markers
Blunt-ended tapestry needle

TENSION
32 sts and 40 rows to 4in (10cm) over
Twisty Rib Patt, after blocking.
28 sts and 32 rows to 4in (10cm) over
st st, after blocking.
Each patt rep is 1¼in (3cm) long.
Use larger or smaller needles if
necessary to obtain correct tension.

PATTERN NOTES
These socks are knitted from the top
down, cast on using the long-tail method
(page 113) and joined with a jogless
join (page 115). The heel flap is worked
in a slip stitch pattern and the instep is
shaped with a gusset (page 130). The
toe stitches are grafted to finish (page
142). You can easily alter the length of
these socks by adding or subtracting
pattern repeats. If you don't want to add
a full repeat, simply continue without
repeating the twist round (rnd 5).

TWISTY RIB
Worked over multiples of 5 sts
and 10 rnds

TWISTY RIB

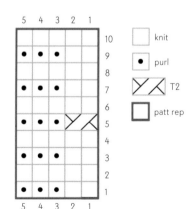

Rnd 1: (K2, p3) to end.
Rnd 2: Knit.
Rnds 3 and 4: Rep rnds 1 and 2
once more.
Rnd 5 (twist): (T2, p3) to end.
Rnd 6: Knit.
Rnds 7-10: Rep rnds 1 and 2.

SOCK (MAKE 2)
Cast on 64 sts. Join to work in the
round, taking care not to twist sts,
and pm to mark beg of rnd.
Rib rnd: (K1 tbl, p1) to end.
Rep rib rnd until cuff meas ¾in (2cm).
Knit 1 rnd, inc 1 st (65 sts).
SET TWISTY RIB
Using Chart or written instructions,
work 4 full reps in Twisty Rib (40 rnds).
On last rnd, a k rnd, work as foll:
K32, pm (halfway point), k15, k2tog,
k to end (64 sts).
HEEL FLAP
Turn and work heel flap back and forth.
Row 1 (WS): Sl1, p to m, turn.
Row 2: (Sl1, k1) to end.
Row 3: As row 1.
Row 4: Sl2, (k1, sl1) to last 2 sts, k2.
These 4 rnds form heel patt and
are repeated.

Cont as set until you have worked eight 4-row reps. Heel flap meas approx 2½in (6cm).

Next row (WS): Purl.

TURN HEEL

Short row 1 (RS): Sl1, k16, ssk, k1, turn. 12 unworked sts rem after gap.

Short row 2 (WS): Sl1, p3, p2tog, p1, turn. 12 unworked sts rem after gap.

Short row 3: Sl1, k to 1 st before gap, ssk, k1, turn.

Short row 4: Sl1, p to 1 st before gap, p2tog, p1, turn.

Rep rows 3 and 4 until all sts have been worked, ending with a WS row. 18 heel sts rem.

GUSSET

Now return to working in the round.

Set-up rnd 1: With RS facing, k18 heel sts, pm for temporary beg of rnd, pick up 16 sts (1 in each slipped st up side of heel flap), pick up 1 st in gap between heel flap and instep, sm (original beg of rnd marker now marks start of instep sts), patt across 32 instep sts as set, sm (end of instep), pick up 17 sts (1 in gap between instep and heel flap and 1 in each slipped st down side of heel flap), k across 18 heel sts to end of rnd (84 sts).

Set-up rnd 2: K tbl to 4 sts before start of instep marker, (ssk) twice, sm, patt across instep sts, sm, (k2tog) twice, k15 tbl, k to end of rnd (80 sts).

Set-up rnd 3: K to m, sm, patt to m, sm, k to end.

Rnd 1: K to 2 sts before m, k2tog, sm, patt to m, sm, ssk, k to end (dec 2).

Rnd 2: K to m, sm, patt to m, sm, k to end.

Rep rnds 1 and 2 until 64 sts rem: 32 each for instep and sole.

Remove temporary beg of rnd marker. From this point the original marker at beg of instep sts will be beg of rnd marker and the second marker at the other end of the instep sts will mark halfway point.

SET FOOT PATT

Rnd 1: Keeping Twisty Rib correct as set, patt to m, sm, k to end.

This rnd sets Twisty Rib patt over instep and st st over sole. Cont as now set until foot meas 9½in (24cm) or 2in (5cm) less than desired length (see Pattern Notes), ending after rnd 10 of Twisty Rib patt. Knit 1 rnd.

SET TOE DECREASES

Rnd 1 (dec): *K1, ssk, k to 3 sts before m, k2tog, k1; sm, rep from * once more (dec 4).

Rnd 2: Knit.

Rep these 2 rnds 7 more times, ending after rnd 2 (32 sts).

Then rep rnd 1 only, 4 more times (16 sts). Divide sts evenly over 2 needles and graft tog.

TO FINISH

Weave in ends.
Block.

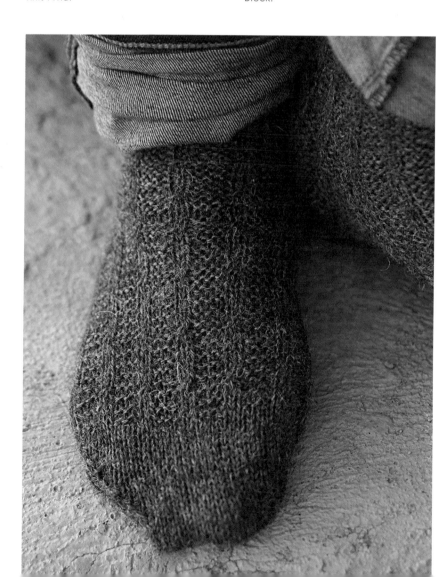

CUCKOO WALK

Inspired by the beautiful South Downs, these cosy DK-weight socks combine a lacy eyelet pattern with a twisty cable.

SIZE
To fit: Adult woman UK 5-7
Cuff circumference: 8¾in (22cm)
Foot length (adjustable): 24cm (9½in)

YOU WILL NEED
West Yorkshire Spinners Fleece DK
100% British Jacobs wool
(approx 254yd/232m per 100g)
1 x 100g hank in 001 Ecru
3.5mm and 4mm double-pointed or circular needles
Stitch markers
Blunt-ended tapestry needle

TENSION
20 sts and 27 rnds to 4in (10cm) over main patt using larger needles.
Use larger or smaller needles if necessary to obtain correct tension.

PATTERN NOTE
These socks are knitted from the top down, cast on using the long-tail method (page 113) and joined with a jogless join (page 115). The heel flap is worked in heel stitch (page 129) and a gusset is worked to shape the foot (page 130). The toe stitches are grafted together to finish (page 142).

SOCK (MAKE 2)
Using 3.5mm needles cast on 44 sts.
Join to work in the round, taking care not to twist sts, and pm to mark beg of rnd.

CUFF
Rnd 1: K1, p1, *k2, (p1, k1) 4 times, p1; rep from * to last 9 sts, k2, (p1, k1) to last st, p1.
Rnd 2: K1, p1, *T2, (p1, k1) 4 times, p1; rep from * to last 9 sts, T2, (p1, k1) to last st, p1.
Rep rnds 1 and 2 two more times.

SET LEG PATT
Change to 4mm needles.
Rnd 1: (P2, k2, p2, k5) around.
Rnd 2: (P2, T2, p2, k2tog, yo, k1, yo, skpo) around.
Rep rows 1 and 2 until piece meas 4¾in (12cm), ending with rnd 1.
Next rnd: Patt as set to last 2 sts, pm. This is the new beg of rnd.

SHAPE HEEL FLAP
Patt 19 sts as set (rnd 1), k2, pm. These 21 sts will be instep sts.
Work back and forth on next 23 sts only for heel flap.
Row 1 (RS): Sl1, k to end, turn.
Row 2: (Sl1, p1) to last st, p1, turn.
Rep these 2 rows until heel flap meas approx 2in (5cm), ending with row 2.

TURN HEEL
Short row 1 (RS): K14, w&t.
Short row 2 (WS): P5, w&t.
Short row 3: K to wrapped st, k wrap tog with wrapped st, w&t.
Short row 4: P to wrapped st, p wrap tog with wrapped st, w&t.
Rep rows 3 and 4 until all sts have been worked, ending with a WS row.

SET GUSSET DECREASES
Turn and work one row along the 23 heel sts on RS, working last wraps tog with their wrapped sts as you come to them.
Pm (temporary beg of rnd marker), pick up and k9 sts along side of heel flap (1 in each slipped stitch and 1 more between side and top of foot), sm, k2, patt rnd 2 to 2 sts before m, k2, sm, pick up 9 sts along side of heel flap (1 between top and side of foot and 1 in each slipped stitch down side of heel flap), k to end.
Rnd 1: K to 4 sts before m, k2tog, T2, sm, k2, patt as set to 2 sts before m2, k2, sm, T2, ssk, k to end.
Rnd 2: K to m, sm, k2, patt as set to 2 sts before m, k2, sm, k to end.
Rep rnds 1 and 2 until 44 sts rem: 21 for instep and 23 for sole, ending with rnd 2.

Remove temporary beg of rnd marker –
rnd now begins at start of instep.
K to new beg of rnd.

SET FOOT PATT

Rnd 1: Patt as set to m, sm, T2, k to last
2 sts, T2.
Rnd 2: Patt as set to m, k to end.
Rep rnds 1 and 2 until foot meas
7½in (19cm) or 2in (5cm) less than
desired length.

SHAPE TOE

Set-up rnd: Patt to m, ssk, k to 2 sts
before end of rnd, k2tog (42 sts: 21 each
on top of foot and sole).
Rnd 1: Knit.
Rnd 2: *K1, ssk, k to 3 sts before m,
k2tog, k1; rep from * once.
Rep rnds 1 and 2 until 30 sts rem, then
work rnd 2 only until 14 sts rem.
Graft toe sts.

TO FINISH

Weave in ends.

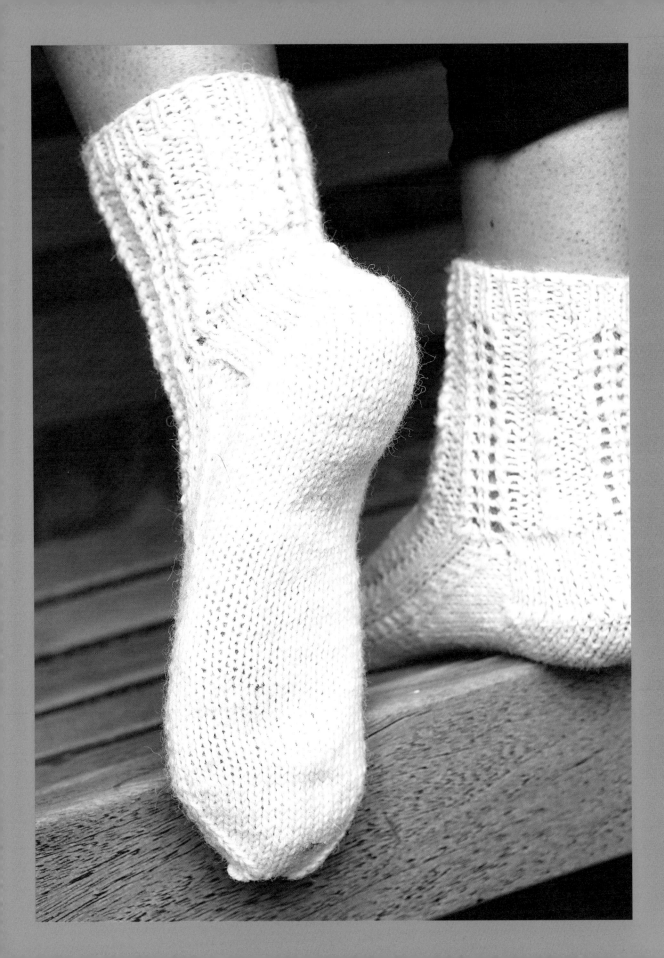

MARY

Intertwined cables snake their way up these cosy and comfortable socks in pretty colour effect yarn.

SIZE

To fit: Adult woman UK 5-7
Cuff circumference: 6¾in (17cm)
Foot length: 9in (23cm) (adjustable)

YOU WILL NEED

Rowan Sock 75% wool, 25% polyamide (approx 437yd/400m per 100g)
1 x 100g ball in 003 Evergreen
2.5mm double-pointed or circular needles
Cable needle
Stitch markers
Scrap yarn

TENSION

32 sts and 45 rnds to 4in (10cm) over st st.
Each patt rep meas approx 1in (2.5cm) long.
Use larger or smaller needles if necessary to obtain correct tension.

PATTERN NOTES

These socks are knitted from the toe up, cast on using Judy's Magic Cast On (page 116). The heel is turned using German short rows (page 133) and the cuff is cast off using Jeny's Surprisingly Stretchy Bind Off (page 146).

TIP

If you don't have a cable needle small enough, use a spare double-pointed needle.

MARY CABLE

Worked over 20 sts and 12 rnds
Rnd 1: P2, k1, (p2, k2) 3 times, p2, k1, p2.
Rnds 2-6: As rnd 1.
Rnd 7: P2, C8Brib, C8Frib, p2.
Rnds 8-12: As rnd 1.

MARY CABLE

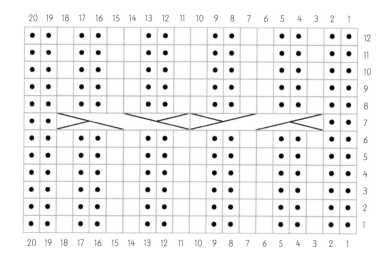

KEY

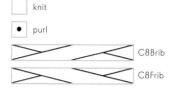

| | knit |
| • | purl |

C8Brib

C8Frib

SOCK (MAKE 2)

Using Judy's Magic Cast On, cast on 24 sts. Pm to mark beg of rnd and after 12 sts for halfway point.

SET TOE SHAPING

Rnd 1: Knit, knitting any twisted sts tbl to untwist them.

Rnd 2 (inc): *K1, kfb, k to 2 sts before halfway m, kfb, k1; sm, rep from * once more (28 sts).

Rnd 3: Rep rnd 2 (32 sts).

Rnd 4: Knit.

Rnd 5 (inc): *K1, m1L, k to last st before halfway m, m1R, k1; sm, rep from * once more (inc 4).

Rnd 6: Knit.

Rep rnds 5 and 6 until you have 60 sts, ending with rnd 6.

Knit 2 rnds.

SET FOOT PATT

Rnd 1 (inc): K7, pm, pfb, k1, pfb, (k2, p2) twice, k2, pfb, k1, pfb, pm, k to end (64 sts).

Rnd 2: K7, sm, work rnd 2 of Mary Cable to m, sm, k to end.

Rnd 2 sets position of foot patt.

Cont in patt as set until you have worked 4 full reps of Mary Cable, and to end of rnd 11 of the following rep.

TURN HEEL

Short row 1 (RS): Patt as set across instep sts (rnd 12 of Mary Cable), k to last st, w&t.

Short row 2 (WS): P to 1 st before halfway marker, w&t.

Short row 3: K to last st before wrapped st, w&t.

Short row 4: P to last st before wrapped st, w&t.

Rep rows 3 and 4 seven more times. 12 sts rem unwrapped between wrapped sts.

Short row 5 (RS): K to first wrapped st, k wrapped st tog with wrap, turn.

Short row 6 (WS): Sl1p, p to first wrapped st, p wrapped st tog with wrap, turn.

Short row 7: Sl1p, k to first wrapped st, k wrapped st tog with wrap, turn.

Short row 8: Sl1p, p to first wrapped st, p wrapped st tog with wrap, turn.

Rep rows 7 and 8 until all wrapped sts have been worked together with their wraps, then k to end of rnd.

Return to working in the round.

SET LEG PATT

Next rnd (inc): Patt as set across instep sts (rnd 1 of Mary Cable), sm, k6, pm, pfb, k1, pfb, (k2, p2) twice, k2, pfb, k1, pfb, pm, k to end (68 sts).

Next rnd: *K7, sm, work rnd 2 of Mary Cable, sm, k to m; rep from * once more. The last rnd sets leg pattern. Cont in patt as set until 9 full reps of Mary Cable have been worked along Sock, ending with rnd 12.

SET CUFF

Next rnd (dec): (K1, p1) 3 times, k1, p2tog, k1, p2tog, (k1, p1) 6 times, k2tog, p2tog, (k1, p1) 3 times; rep from * once more (60 sts).

Rib rnd: (K1, p1) around.

Rep rib rnd another 8 times.

Cast off using Jeny's Surprisingly Stretchy Bind Off.

TO FINISH

Weave in ends.

DAY-GLO

There's nothing like a bit of neon in your knitting, and these funky socks in a two-colour brioche pattern are the perfect addition to any wardrobe.

SIZES

To fit: Baby age 0-6mths
[Adult UK size 5-7]
Cuff circumference: 4[8]in (10[20]cm)
Foot length: 3¼[9]in (8[23]cm)
Figures in square brackets refer to larger sizes: where there is only one set of figures this refers to all sizes.

YOU WILL NEED

Opal Uni 4 Ply 75% superwash wool, 25% polyamide
(approx 465yd/425m per 100g)
1 x 100g ball in 2010 Neon Pink (A)
1 x 100g ball in 2012 Neon Yellow (B)
1 x 100g ball in 3081 Natural (C)
2.5mm double-pointed needles
Stitch markers
Note: These yarn amounts are plenty to knit both sizes, size 1 uses only small amounts of each shade.

TENSION

30 sts and 42 rnds to 4in (10cm) over st st.
25 sts and 68 rnds to 4in (10cm) over two-colour brioche stitch.
49 sts and 68 rnds to 4in (10cm) over two-colour slip-st patt.
Use larger or smaller needles if necessary to obtain correct tension.

PATTERN NOTES

These socks are knitted from the toe up, cast on using Judy's Magic Cast On (page 116), with the main instep pattern worked in two-colour brioche (page 139) and the sole worked in a simple slip stitch pattern for extra endurance. The heel is turned using shadow-wrap short rows (page 132) and the cuff is cast off using a stretchy cast off (page 145). Two-colour brioche is reversible, so wear with the cuffs folded over.

SOCK (MAKE 2)

Using A and Judy's Magic Cast On, cast on 12[24] sts.
Working any twisted sts tbl to untwist them, work as foll: pm to mark beg of rnd, k6[12], pm to mark halfway point, k to end.

SET TOE INCREASES

Inc rnd: *Sm, k1, kfb, k to 2 sts before halfway m, kfb, k1; rep from * to end (inc 4).
Rep inc rnd twice more. 24[36] sts.
**Knit 1 rnd.
Rep inc rnd. 28[40] sts.
Rep from ** once more. 32[44] sts.

SIZE 2 ONLY

***Knit 2 rnds.
Rep inc rnd (48 sts).
Rep from *** 3 more times (60 sts).

BOTH SIZES

Knit 1 rnd. Break A.

SET FOOT PATTERN

Next rnd: Using B, k to halfway m, dec 3[5] sts evenly (13[25] sts in first half for instep); sm, k to end, inc 9[19] sts evenly (25[49] sts in second half for sole). 38[74] sts total.

Instep set-up rnd: Using C, (k1, sl1yo) to last st before m, k1, sm, (k1, sl1 wyib) to last st, k1.

Rnd 1: Using B, sl1 wyib, (brp1, sl1yo) to last 2 sts before m, brp1, sl1 wyib, sm, (sl1 wyib, k1) to last st, sl1 wyib.

Rnd 2: Using C, k1, (sl1yo, brk1) to last st before m, k1, sm, (k1, sl1 wyib) to last st, k1.

Rep rnds 1 and 2 until foot meas 2½[7]in (6[18]cm) or ¾[2]in (2[5]cm) less than desired length, ending after rnd 2.

TURN HEEL

Set-up rnd: Using B, patt across instep sts as set, sm, k across sole sts, dec 9[19] sts evenly (16[30] sts for sole). 29[55] sts.

Join A but do not break B and C.
Cont in A for all of heel turn as foll:
Turn and work on WS of sole sts.
Short row 1 (WS): P to last st, w&t.
Short row 2 (RS): K to last st, w&t.
Short row 3: P to last st before

wrapped st, w&t.

Short row 4: K to last st before wrapped st, w&t.

Rep short rows 3 and 4 until 6[12] sts remain unwrapped, ending after row 4.

Short row 5 (WS): Sl1, p to first wrapped st, p wrap tog with wrapped st, turn.

Short row 6: Sl1, k to next wrapped st, k wrap tog with wrapped st, turn.

Rep rows 5 and 6 until all wrapped sts have been worked.

Next row (WS): P to halfway m, break A. Using B, k to end, dec 3[5] sts evenly across (13[25] sts in second half). 26[50] sts total.

Now return to working in the round.

LEG

Set-up rnd: Using C, k1, (brk1, sl1yo) to last st before halfway marker, k1, remove marker, (sl1yo, k1) to last st, sl1yo.

Rnd 1: Using B, (sl1yo, brp1) around.

Rnd 2: Using C, (brk1, sl1yo) around.

Rep rnds 1 and 2 until leg meas 1½[5]in (4[12.5]cm) from top of heel or ¼[½]in (0.5[1]cm) less than desired length, ending after rnd 2.

SET CUFF

Next rnd: Using B, p to end.

Break B and C and cont in A only.

Purl 3[5] rnds.

Cast off using a stretchy cast off.

TO FINISH

Weave in ends and close up any tiny holes at the heel.

HOOF AND CLAW

Two complementary cables adorn this classic sock in British racing green.

SIZE

To fit: Average man UK 10-12
Cuff circumference: 8¾in (22cm)
Foot length: 9¾in (25cm) (adjustable)

YOU WILL NEED

SweetGeorgia Tough Love Sock
80% superwash Merino wool, 20% nylon
(approx 424yd/388m per 115g skein)
1 x 115g skein in Racing Green
2mm and 2.25mm double-pointed or
circular needles
Cable needle
Stitch markers
Blunt-ended tapestry needle

TENSION

31 sts and 46 rnds to 4in (10cm) over
st st using 2.25mm needles.
36 sts and 36 rnds to 4in (10cm) over rib
using 2mm needles.
*Use larger or smaller needles if
necessary to obtain correct tension.*

PATTERN NOTES

These socks are knitted from the top
down, cast on using the long-tail method
(page 113) and joined using a jogless join
(page 115). A slip stitch heel flap (page
129) and a gusset (page 130) are worked.
The toes are grafted to finish (page 142).

TIPS

This pattern divides neatly into four so
works well over four dpns. If you don't
have a small enough cable needle, use
a spare dpn.

MINI-CLAW CABLE

Worked over 9 sts and 4 rnds
Row 1: Knit.
Row 2 and every alt row: Knit.
Row 3: C4R, k1, C4L.

MINI CLAW CABLE

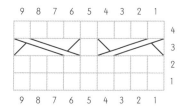

HORSESHOE CABLE

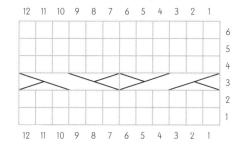

HORSESHOE CABLE

Worked over 12 sts and 6 rnds
Row 1: Knit.
Row 2 and every alt row: Knit.
Row 3: C6B, C6F.
Row 5: Knit.

SOCK (MAKE 2)

Using 2mm needles, cast on 80 sts.
Join in the rnd taking care not to twist
sts. Pm for beg of rnd and after 40 sts.

KEY

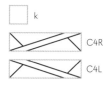

KEY

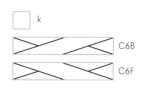

Rib rnd: (K1, p1) around.

Rep rib rnd until piece meas 1in (2.5cm).

SET MAIN PATTERN

Change to bigger needles.

Rnd 1: **K1, *p2, work row 1 of Mini-claw Cable, p2*, work row 1 of Horseshoe Cable, rep from * to *, k1; sm, rep from ** to end.

This rnd sets leg patt. Cont as set for 15 full reps of Mini-claw Cable and 10 full reps of Horseshoe Cable.

HEEL FLAP

Next rnd: Cont in patt as set to end of rnd, then turn and work on second half of sts only.

Row 1 (WS): Sl1 kwise, p39, turn.

Row 2 (RS): (Sl1, k1) to end.

Rep these 2 rows 17 more times, then row 1 once more.

SHAPE HEEL

Short row 1 (RS): Sl1, k21, ssk, k1, turn.

Short row 2 (WS): Sl1, p5, p2tog, p1, turn.

Short row 3: Sl1, k to last st before gap, ssk, k1, turn.

Short row 4: Sl1, p to last st before gap, p2tog, p1, turn.

Rep rows 3 and 4 another 6 times.

Short row 5 (RS): Sl1, k20, k2tog, turn.

Short row 6 (WS): Sl1, p20, p2tog, turn.

GUSSET

Next rnd (rejoin in the rnd): K22 across sole, pm at this point for temporary new beg of rnd, pick up and k19 sts up side of heel flap, work 40 instep sts in patt as set, pick up and k19 sts down side of heel flap, k across 22 sole sts to temporary beg of rnd marker (100 sts).

Set-up rnd: K16 tbl, k2tog, move original beg of rnd marker to this point, k2tog (last picked-up st with first instep st), patt as set to last instep st, ssk (last instep st with first picked-up st), move halfway m to this point, ssk, k16 tbl, k to end (96 sts).

Rnd 1: K to m, sm, work instep sts in patt as set, sm, k to end.

Rnd 2: K to 2 sts before m, k2tog, sm, work instep sts in patt as set, sm, ssk, k to end (dec 2).

Rep rnds 1 and 2 until you have 80 sts: 40 across instep worked in patt as set and 40 sts in st st for sole.

Note: Beg of rnd now returns to start of instep sts. Remove temporary beg of rnd marker.

FOOT

Rnd 1: Patt across 40 instep sts, sm, k to end.

Rnd 1 sets patt for foot with patt over instep and st st over sole.

Cont as set until you have worked a total of 33 full reps of Mini-claw Cable and 22 full reps of Horseshoe Cable.

Foot meas approx 8in (20.5cm).

Note: To adjust foot length, work fewer or more pattern repeats before working toe. End with rnd 6 of Horseshoe Cable. If you extend the length you may need additional yarn.

SHAPE TOE

Knit 1 rnd.

Rnd 1: *K1, ssk, k to 3 sts before m, k2tog, k1; rep from * to end (76 sts).

Rnds 2-4: Knit.

Rep rnds 1-4 twice (68 sts).

Then work rnd 1 every alt rnd until
36 sts remain.
Graft rem sts together.

TO FINISH
Weave in ends and block.

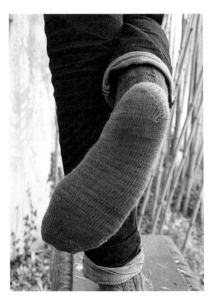

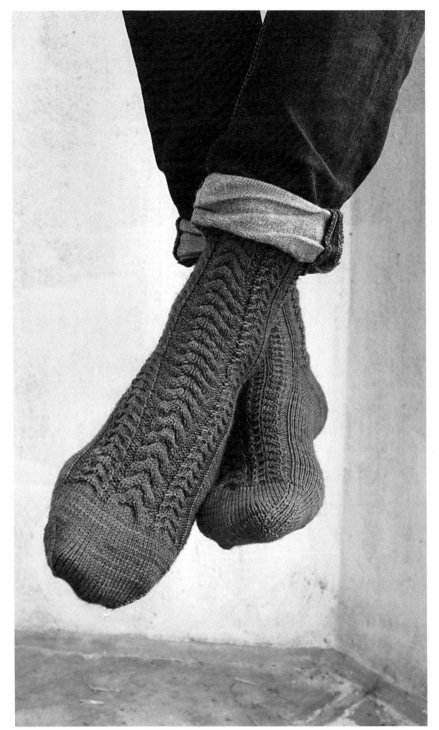

HARUKI

These cute mini-socks feature a Japanese stitch pattern and are named for one of my favourite Japanese authors, Haruki Murakami.

SIZES
To fit: UK size 4-6[7-9]
Cuff circumference: 7¾[8¼]in (19.5[22]cm)
Foot length: 8¼[9½]in (21[25]cm)
Figures in square brackets refer to larger sizes: where there is only one set of figures this applies to all sizes.

YOU WILL NEED
EasyKnits Deeply Wicked
100% superwash Merino wool (approx 437yd/400m per 100g)
1 x 100g skein in Limey
2.5mm double-pointed or circular needles
Stitch markers

TENSION
32 sts and 44 rnds to 4in (10cm) over st st.
Each 28-rnd Lace Patt rep meas 2½in (6cm).
Use larger or smaller needles if necessary to obtain correct tension.

PATTERN NOTES
These socks are knitted from the toe up and cast on using Judy's Magic Cast On (page 116). The heel is turned using German short rows (page 133) and the cuff is cast off using the stretchy method (page 145). To make the socks shorter or longer, work fewer or more full patt reps before working the final rnds 1-12. You can turn the heel at any point in the lace pattern to suit your foot length and desired leg length. The heel meas approx 1½[2]in (4[5]cm), so take this into account when adjusting length.

LACE PATT
Worked over 31 sts and 28 rnds
Rnd 1: K2, *p2, sl1p wyib, p2*, yo, k3, ssk, k3, k1 tbl, k3, k2tog, k3, yo; rep from * to *, k2.
Rnd 2: K2, **p2, k1, p2**, k1, yo, k3, ssk, k2, k1 tbl, k2, k2tog, k3, yo, k1; rep from ** to **, k2.
Rnd 3: K2, work from * to * as row 1, k2, yo, k3, ssk, k1, k1 tbl, k1, k2tog, k3, yo, k2; rep from * to *, k2.
Rnd 4: K2, work from ** to ** as row 2, k3, yo, k3, ssk, k1 tbl, k2tog, k3, yo, k3; rep from ** to **, k2.
Rnds 5-12: Rep rnds 1-4 twice.
Rnd 13: K2, work from * to * as row 1, yo, k7, sk2po, k7, yo; rep from * to *, k2.
Rnds 14, 16, 18, 20, 22, 24 and 26: K2, work from ** to ** as row 2, k17, rep from ** to **, k2.
Rnd 15: K2, work from * to * as row 1, k1, yo, k6, sk2po, k6, yo, k1; rep from * to *, k2.
Rnd 17: K2, work from * to * as row 1, k2, yo, k5, sk2po, k5, yo, k2; rep from * to *, k2.
Rnd 19: K2, work from * to * as row 1, k3, yo, k4, sk2po, k4, yo, k3; rep from * to *, k2.
Rnd 21: K2, work from * to * as row 1, k4, yo, k3, sk2po, k3, yo, k4; rep from * to *, k2.
Rnd 23: K2, work from * to * as row 1, k5, yo, k2, sk2po, k2, yo, k5; rep from * to *, k2.
Rnd 25: K2, work from * to * as row 1, k6, yo, k1, sk2po, k1, yo, k6; rep from * to *, k2.
Rnd 27: K2, work from * to * as row 1, k7, yo, sk2po, yo, k7; rep from * to *, k2.
Rnd 28: K2, work from ** to ** as row 2, k17; rep from ** to **, k2.

SOCK (MAKE 2)
Cast on 26 sts using Judy's Magic Cast On. Pm to mark beg of rnd and after 13 sts for halfway point.
Knit 1 rnd, working any twisted sts tbl to untwist them.
Next rnd (inc): *Sm, k1, m1L, k to 1 st before m, m1R, k1; rep from * once more (inc 4).

Next rnd: Knit.

Rep last 2 rnds 3[5] more times, then rep inc rnd every 3rd rnd until you have 62[70] sts, ending with a straight rnd.

SET LACE PATT

Rnd 1: Working from Chart or written instructions, k0[2], work row 1 Lace Patt, k to end.

This rnd sets position of Lace Patt. Cont as set until foot meas 1½[2]in (4[5]cm) less than desired length.

Size 1 (pictured) ends on rnd 28 after 2 full reps of lace patt. Size 2 works another half patt rep after this, ending on rnd 12.

TURN HEEL

Turn and work German short rows in rev st st across heel sts only as foll:

Short row 1 (WS): Sl1p, pull working yarn so the two legs of the st sit on the needle, k next st firmly, k to halfway marker, turn.

Short row 2 (RS): Sl1p, pull on the working yarn so the two legs of the st sit on the needle, k next st firmly, p to first wrapped st, turn.

CHART

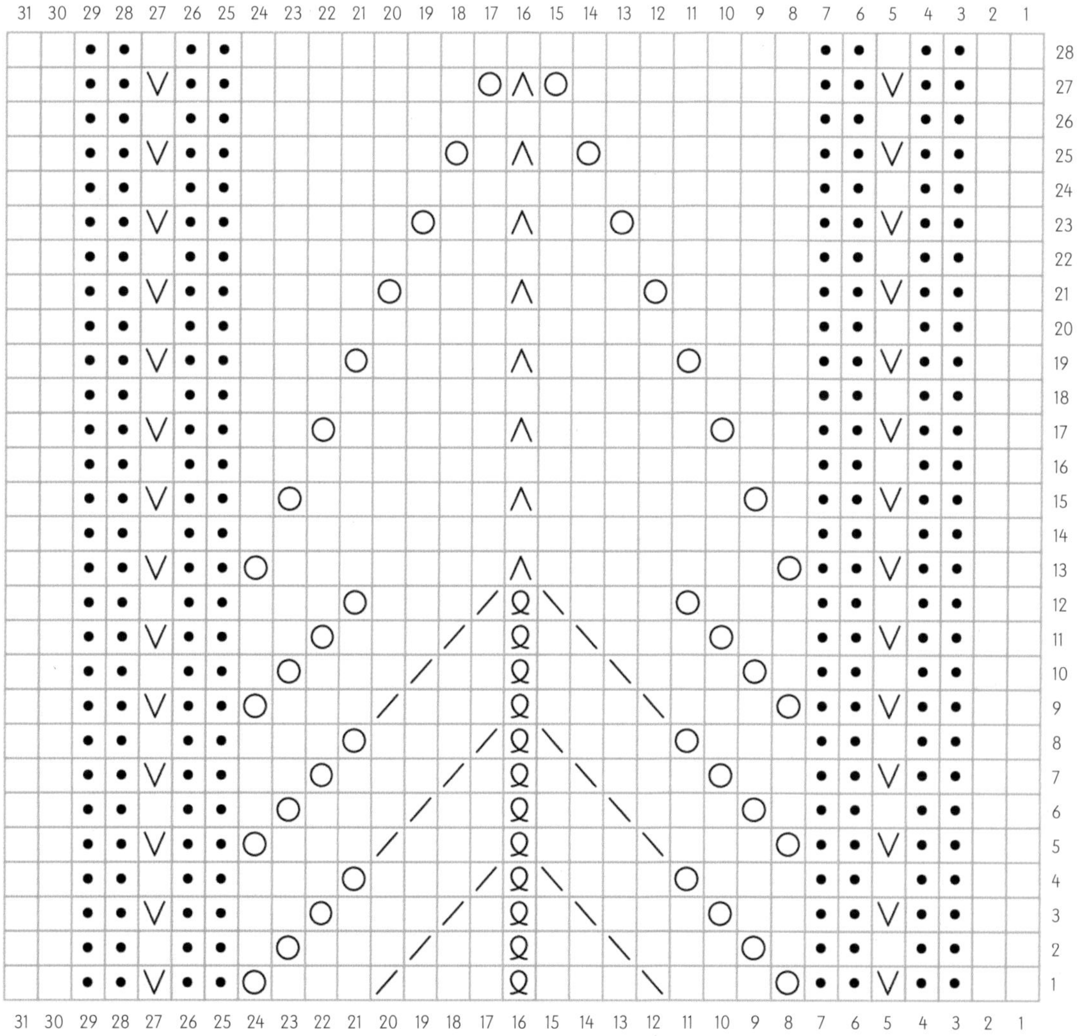

31	30	29	28	27	26	25	24	23	22	21	20	19	18	17	16	15	14	13	12	11	10	9	8	7	6	5	4	3	2	1	Rnd
		•	•		•	•																		•	•		•	•			28
		•	•	V	•	•							O	Λ	O									•	•	V	•	•			27
		•	•		•	•																		•	•		•	•			26
		•	•	V	•	•						O		Λ		O								•	•	V	•	•			25
		•	•		•	•																		•	•		•	•			24
		•	•	V	•	•					O			Λ			O							•	•	V	•	•			23
		•	•		•	•																		•	•		•	•			22
		•	•	V	•	•				O				Λ				O						•	•	V	•	•			21
		•	•		•	•																		•	•		•	•			20
		•	•	V	•	•			O					Λ					O					•	•	V	•	•			19
		•	•		•	•																		•	•		•	•			18
		•	•	V	•	•		O						Λ						O				•	•	V	•	•			17
		•	•		•	•																		•	•		•	•			16
		•	•	V	•	•	O							Λ							O			•	•	V	•	•			15
		•	•		•	•																		•	•		•	•			14
		•	•	V	•	•	O							Λ								O		•	•	V	•	•			13
		•	•		•	•	O	/						Ω						\	O			•	•		•	•			12
		•	•	V	•	•	O	/						Ω						\	O			•	•	V	•	•			11
		•	•		•	•	O		/					Ω					\		O			•	•		•	•			10
		•	•	V	•	•	O		/					Ω					\		O			•	•	V	•	•			9
		•	•		•	•	O			/				Ω				\			O			•	•		•	•			8
		•	•	V	•	•	O			/				Ω				\			O			•	•	V	•	•			7
		•	•		•	•	O				/			Ω			\				O			•	•		•	•			6
		•	•	V	•	•	O				/			Ω			\				O			•	•	V	•	•			5
		•	•		•	•	O					/		Ω		\					O			•	•		•	•			4
		•	•	V	•	•	O					/		Ω		\					O			•	•	V	•	•			3
		•	•		•	•	O						/	Ω	\						O			•	•		•	•			2
		•	•	V	•	•	O						/	Ω	\						O			•	•	V	•	•			1

KEY

- ☐ k
- • p
- O yo
- \ ssk
- / k2tog
- Λ sk2po
- V sl1p wyib
- Ω k tbl

Short row 3: Sl1p, pull on the working yarn so the two legs of the st sit on the needle, k next st firmly, k to wrapped st, turn.

Rep rows 2 and 3 until 13 sts rem unwrapped, ending after a WS row 3.

Short row 4 (RS): Sl1p, p to first wrapped st, p tog the 2 legs of the wrapped st, turn.

Short row 5 (WS): Sl1p, k to first wrapped st, k tog the 2 legs of the wrapped st, turn.

Rep last 2 rows until all wrapped sts have been worked tog, then p to end of rnd ready to continue in the rnd.

LEG

You will now work in the round for the leg.

Rnd 1 (dec): Work rnd 1[13] of Lace Patt from Chart or written instructions, sm, (p2, sl1p wyib) to last 1[2] sts, m1p[p1], p1. 63[70] sts.

Rnd 2: Work rnd 2[14] of Lace Patt, sm, (p2, k1) to last 2 sts, p2.

Rnd 3: Work rnd 3[15] of Lace Patt, sm, (p2, sl1p) to last 2 sts, p2.

These 2 rnds set position of Lace Patt front and slip-stitch rib back of leg.

Cont in patt as set until you have worked 3[4] full reps of Lace Patt or number of reps until leg meas 2in (5cm) less than desired length, then work rnds 1-12 only.

SET RIB

Next rnd: (P1, k1) 1[2] times, (p2, k1) 4 times, p1, k1, p1, (k1, p2) 4 times, (k1, p1) 1[2] times, sm, k1, p1, (k1, p2) 9[10] times to last 3 sts, k1, p1, k1.

This rnd forms rib. Rep rib rnd 9 more times.

Cast off using a stretchy method.

TO FINISH

Weave in ends.

Block to open out lace.

STAR FISHING

Hot pink stars streak across the sparkly night sky of these fabulous socks, adorned with a pretty lace pattern and worked with a heel flap and gusset.

SIZE
To fit: Average woman UK 5-7
Cuff circumference: 5½in (14cm)
Foot length: 9½in (24cm) (adjustable)

YOU WILL NEED
Banshee Yarns RuPaul Inspired Socks
in shade Uniqueness
100g in 75% superwash Merino wool,
20% nylon, 5% silver Stellina sparkle
(approx 437yd/400m per 100g) (A)
20g in 75% superwash Merino wool, 25%
nylon (approx 93yd/85m per 20g) (B)
2.5mm double-pointed or circular needles
Stitch markers

TENSION
32 sts and 45 rnds to 4in (10cm)
over st st.
Use larger or smaller needles if
necessary to obtain correct tension.

PATTERN NOTES
These socks are knitted from the toe
up, cast on using Judy's Magic Cast
On (page 116). The heel is turned using
German short rows (see page 133). The
cuff is cast off using Jeny's Surprisingly
Stretchy Bind Off (page 146).
The yarn featured in the sample is no
longer available: try West Yorkshire
Spinners Signature Sock Sparkle or
search 'sparkle sock yarn' for alternatives.

LACE LADDER
Worked over 6 sts and 4 rnds
Rnd 1: P2, yo, ssk, p2.
Rnd 2: P2, k2, p2.
Rnd 3: P2, k2tog, yo, p2.
Rnd 4: Rep rnd 2.

LACE LADDER

						KEY
						knit
						• purl
						◯ yo
						╲ ssk
						╱ k2tog

HEART VINE LACE
Worked over 11 sts and 10 rnds
Rnd 1: K2, yo, k1, k2tog, p1, ssk, k1, yo, k2.
Rnd 2 and all alt rnds: K5, p1, k5.
Rnd 3: Rep rnd 1.
Rnd 5: K3, k2tog, yo, p1, yo, ssk, k3.

HEART VINE LACE

KEY
knit
• purl
◯ yo
╱ k2tog
╲ ssk

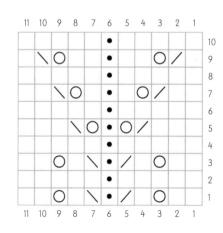

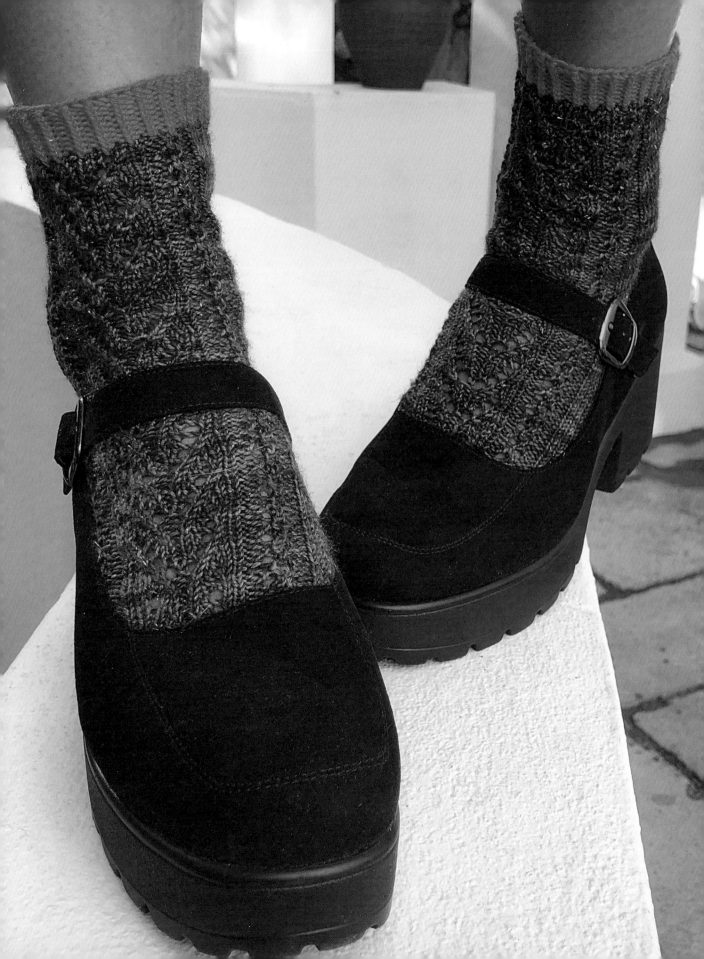

Rnd 7: K2, k2tog, yo, k1, p1, k1, yo, ssk, k2.
Rnd 9: K1, k2tog, yo, k2, p1, k2, yo, ssk, k1.
Rnd 10: Rep rnd 2.

SOCK (MAKE 2)

Using B and Judy's Magic Cast On, cast on 24 sts. Pm to mark beg of rnd and after 12 sts for halfway point.

SET TOE SHAPING

Rnd 1: Knit, working any twisted sts tbl to untwist them.
Rnd 2 (inc): *K1, kfb, k to 2 sts before halfway m, kfb, k1; sm, rep from * once more (28 sts).
Rnd 3: Rep rnd 2 (32 sts).

Rnd 4: Knit.
Rnd 5 (inc): *K1, m1L, k to last st before halfway m, m1R, k1; sm, rep from * once more (inc 4).
Rnd 6: Knit.
Rep rnds 5 and 6 until you have 60 sts, ending after rnd 5. If using dpns, divide over 4 dpns when it is comfortable to do so.
Next rnd: *K14, kfb, k to m; sm, rep from * once more (62 sts).

SET FOOT PATT

Change to A.
Knit 1 rnd.
Rnd 1: K4, work rnd 1 of Lace Ladder

over next 6 sts, work rnd 1 of Heart Vine Lace over next 11 sts, work rnd 1 of Lace Ladder over next 6 sts, k to end.
This rnd sets lace pattern over instep and st st over sole.
Cont in patt as set until you have worked 4 full patt reps of Heart Vine Lace, then work rnds 1-6 again.

SET GUSSET

Rnd 1 (inc): Patt across instep to halfway marker, sm, m1R, pm, k to end of rnd, pm, m1L (64 sts).
Rnd 2: Patt instep sts, k to end.
Rnd 3 (inc): Patt across instep sts, sm, m1R, k to end of rnd slipping markers, m1L (inc 2).
Rnd 4: Patt instep sts, k to end.
Rep rnds 3 and 4 a further 10 times (86 sts – 12 for each gusset).

TURN HEEL

Using A, patt to start of sole sts, slipping markers.
Break A and change to B.
Short row 1 (RS): K to last sole st, w&t.
Short row 2 (WS): P to last st before m, w&t.
Short row 3: K to last st before wrapped st, w&t.
Short row 4: P to last st before wrapped st, w&t.
Rep short rows 3 and 4 a further 7 times until 13 sts rem unwrapped.

SET HEEL FLAP

Row 1 (RS): Working any wrapped sts tog with wraps as you come to them, k to last sole st, remove marker, ssk (last sole st with first gusset st), pm, turn.
Row 2 (WS): Sl1 wyif, working any wrapped sts tog with their wraps as you come to them, p to last sole st, remove marker, p2tog (last sole st with first gusset st), pm, turn.

Row 3: Sl1 wyib, k to last sole st, remove marker, ssk (last sole st with first gusset st), pm, turn.

Row 4: Sl1 wyif, p to last sole st, remove marker, p2tog (last sole st with first gusset st), pm, turn.

Rep rows 3 and 4 until 1 gusset st remains on each side.

Change to A.

With RS facing, sl1 wyib, k to last sole st, remove marker, ssk (last sole st with last gusset st), patt as set across instep sts, k tog last gusset st with first sole st, k to end of sole sts (62 sts).

SET LEG

Rnd 1: *K4, patt as set across Lace Ladders and Heart Vine Lace panel, k4; rep from *, working the same row of Lace Ladders and Heart Vine Lace panel on back leg as on front.

This rnd sets leg lace patt.

Cont in patt as set until you have worked a total of 11 full reps of Heart Vine Lace patt over front of foot, or until leg meas approx 1in (2.5cm) less than desired length, ending with rnd 10 of Heart Vine Lace patt.

SET CUFF

Break A, rejoin B.

Knit 1 rnd.

Rib rnd: (K1 tbl, p1) around.

Rep rib rnd 7 more times.

Cast off using Jeny's Surprisingly Stretchy Bind Off.

TO FINISH

Weave in ends and block according to yarn band instructions.

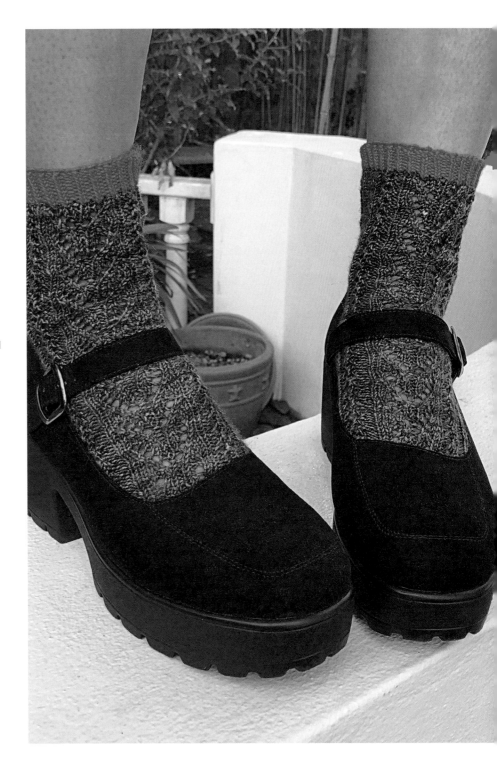

SOMETHING BLUE FOR THE GROOM

Something old, something new, something borrowed and something blue aren't just for the bride. When my best male friend got married in Ireland, these are the new, blue socks I designed specially for him.

SIZE
To fit: Average man UK 9-11.
Foot length: 9¾in (24.5cm)
Foot length may be increased by extending st st section before toe shaping.

YOU WILL NEED
SweetGeorgia Tough Love Sock
80% Merino wool, 20% nylon (approx 424yd/388m per 115g)
1 x 115g hank in 05 Nightshade
2mm and 2.25mm double-pointed or circular needles
Cable needle
2 stitch markers
Blunt-ended tapestry needle

TENSION
34 sts and 49 rows to 4in (10cm) over st st using 2.25mm needles.
Use larger or smaller needles if necessary to obtain correct tension.

PATTERN NOTES
These socks are knitted from the top down, cast on using the long-tail method (page 113) and joined with a jogless join (page 115). The heel is strengthened with a slip stitch pattern (page 129) and the foot shaped with a gusset (page 130). Toes are grafted to finish (page 142). The sample used almost exactly one hank of yarn, so it might be worth getting two just in case. Stitch count varies over cable pattern.

CELTIC LOVE KNOT CABLE
Worked starting and ending with 39 sts and over 44 rnds
Rnd 1: P3, Cr3R, p2, Cr3L, p6, k2, Cr3L, p6, Cr3R, p2, Cr3L, p3.
Rnd 2 and all alt rnds: Work each st as it appears, so k the k sts and p the p sts.
Rnd 3: P2, Cr3R, p4, Cr3L, p4, Cr3R, p1, Cr3L, p4, Cr3R, p4, Cr3L, p2.
Rnd 5: P2, k2, p6, Cr3L, p2, Cr3R, p3, Cr3L, p2, Cr3R, p6, k2, p2.
Rnd 7: P2, k2, p7, Cr3L, Cr3R, p5, Cr3L, Cr3R, p7, k2, p2.
Rnd 9: P2, k2, p8, C4B, p7, C4B, p8, k2, p2.
Rnd 11: P2, Cr3L, p6, Cr3R, Cr3L, p5, Cr3R, Cr3L, p6, Cr3R, p2.
Rnd 13: P3, Cr3L, p4, Cr3R, p2, Cr3L, p3, Cr3R, p2, Cr3L, p4, Cr3R, p3.

Rnd 15: P4, Cr3L, p2, Cr3R, p4, Cr3L, p1, Cr3R, p4, Cr3L, p2, Cr3R, p4.
Rnd 17: P5, Cr3L, Cr3R, p6, Cr3L, k2tog, p6, Cr3L, Cr3R, p5 (38 sts).
Rnd 19: P6, C4F, C3L, p7, C4F, p6.
Rnd 21: P5, Cr3R, Cr3L, p6, k2, Cr3L, pfb, p4, Cr3R, Cr3L, p5 (39 sts).
Rnd 23: P4, Cr3R, p2, Cr3L, p4, Cr3R, p1, Cr3L, p4, Cr3R, p2, Cr3L, p4.
Rnd 25: P3, Cr3R, p4, Cr3L, p2, Cr3R, p3, Cr3L, p2, Cr3R, p4, Cr3L, p3.
Rnd 27: P2, Cr3R, p6, Cr3L, Cr3R, p5, Cr3L, Cr3R, p6, Cr3L, p2.
Rnd 29: Rep rnd 9.
Rnd 31: P2, k2, p7, Cr3R, Cr3L, p5, Cr3R, Cr3L, p7, k2, p2.
Rnd 33: P2, k2, p6, Cr3R, p2, Cr3L, p3, Cr3R, p2, Cr3L, p6, k2, p2.
Rnd 35: P2, Cr3L, p4, Cr3R, p4, Cr3L, p1, Cr3R, p4, Cr3L, p4, Cr3R, p2.
Rnd 37: P3, Cr3L, p2, Cr3R, p6, Cr3L, k2tog, p6, Cr3L, p2, Cr3R, p3 (38 sts).
Rnd 39: P4, Cr3L, Cr3R, p8, sssk, p7, Cr3L, Cr3R, p4 (36 sts).
Rnd 41: P5, C4F, p9, k1, p8, C4F, p5.
Rnd 43: P4, Cr3R, Cr3L, p8, kyok, pfb, p6, Cr3R, Cr3L, p4 (39 sts).
Rnd 44: Work each st as it appears.

SOCK (MAKE 2)

Using 2mm needles cast on 80 sts using the long-tail method. Join to work in the round, taking care not to twist sts, and pm to mark beg of rnd and after 40 sts for halfway point.

SET RIB

Rnd 1: (K1, p1) around.

Rep rib rnd until cuff meas approx 1in (2.5cm).

SET CELTIC LOVE KNOT CABLE

Change to 2.25mm needles.

Set-up rnd 1 (RS): P1, p2tog, p3, k4, p9, ssk, p9, k4, p3, p2tog, p1, sm, p3, (k4, p6) 3 times, k4, p3 (77 sts: 37 across front of leg and 40 across back).

Set-up rnd 2: P5, k4, p9, k1, p9, k4, p5, sm, p3, (k4, p6) 3 times, k4, p3.

Set-up rnd 3: P4, Cr3R, Cr3L, p8, kyok, p8, Cr3R, Cr3L, p4, sm, p3, (k4, p6) 3 times, k4, p3 (79 sts).

Set-up rnd 4: P4, k2, p2, k2, p8, k3, p8, k2, p2, k2, p4, sm, p3, (k4, p6) 3 times, k4, p3.

Work Celtic Love Knot Cable patt from Chart or written instructions across front and rib for back of leg as foll:

Rnd 1: Work rnd 1 of Celtic Love Knot Cable, sm, p3, (k4, p6) 3 times, k4, p3.

Rnd 2: Work rnd 2 of Celtic Love Knot Cable, sm, p3, (k4, p6) 3 times, k4, p3.

These 2 rnds set position of Celtic Love Knot Cable patt and back rib. Cont in patt as set until you have worked rnd 8 of Celtic Love Knot Cable patt.

Cable rnd 1: Work rnd 9 of Celtic Love Knot Cable patt, sm, p3, (C4B, p6) 3 times, C4B, p3.

Cable rnd 2: Work rnd 10 of Celtic Love Knot Cable patt, sm, p3, (k4, p6) 3 times, k4, p3.

CHART

Cont in patt as set until you have worked rnd 18 of Celtic Love Knot Cable patt, then rep cable rnds 1 and 2 but working rnds 19 and 20 of Celtic Love Knot Cable patt.

Cont in patt as set to end of Celtic Love Knot Cable patt, then work rnds 1-16 again, and AT THE SAME TIME work cable rnds 1 and 2 on rnds 29 and 30, then on rnds 39 and 40, then on rnds 5 and 6.

HEEL FLAP

Next rnd: Patt to end of rnd, turn and work on the first 40 sts only for heel flap.

Row 1 (WS): Sl1 kwise, p39, turn.

Row 2: (Sl1, k1) to end.

Rep last 2 rows 17 more times, then row 1 once more.

SHAPE HEEL

Short row 1 (RS): Sl1, k21, ssk, k1, turn.

Short row 2 (WS): Sl1, p5, p2tog, p1, turn.

KEY

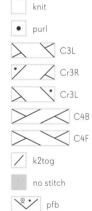

	knit
•	purl
	C3L
	Cr3R
	Cr3L
	C4B
	C4F
	k2tog
	no stitch
	pfb
	sssk
	kyok

Short row 3: Sl1, k to last st before gap, ssk, k1, turn.

Short row 4: Sl1, p to last st before gap, p2tog, p1, turn.

Rep rows 3 and 4 another 6 times.

Row 17: Sl1, k20, ssk, turn.

Row 18: Sl1, p20, p2tog, turn (22 sole sts).

SHAPE GUSSET

Next rnd: Rejoin in the rnd as foll: k22 across sole, pm, pick up and k19 sts up heel flap, sm, patt as set across instep, pm, pick up and k19 down heel flap, pm (99 sts).

Set-up rnd: K22 sole sts, sm, k16 tbl, k2tog, move marker to this point, p2tog (last picked up st with first instep st), patt as set to last instep st, p2tog (last instep st and first st from side of heel flap), move marker to this point, ssk, k16 tbl, k22 sole sts. This is the new start and end of rnd (95 sts).

Rnd 1: K15, k2tog, sm, patt as set across instep sts, sm, ssk, k to end of rnd (93 sts).

Rnd 2: K to instep marker, sm, patt across instep sts, k to end of rnd.

Rnd 3 and every alt rnd (dec): K to last 2 sts before m, k2tog, patt as set across instep sts, sm, ssk, k to end of rnd.

Rnds 2 and 3 set gusset decrease patt. Cont as set until 79 sts rem: 39 across instep, 9 on each side of heel flap, 22 across sole.

On last rnd remove all markers except original markers which are now at beg and end of instep sts.

FOOT

Next rnd: Patt as set across instep sts, k to end.

This rnd sets foot pattern. Cont as set until you have worked 2 full reps of Celtic Love Knot Cable, then to rnd 42 of a third rep.

Next 2 rnds: Work each st as it appears.

Next 2 rnds: P36, k40.

Next rnd: Knit, adjusting sts so you have an equal number of sts for sole and top of foot. Move markers to new beg and middle of rnd.

Note: If you wish to lengthen foot, cont in st st until foot meas 2in (5cm) less than desired length. You may need more yarn if you lengthen the foot.

SHAPE TOE

Rnd 1: (Sm, k1, ssk, k to 3 sts before m, k2tog, k1) twice (72 sts).

Rnds 2-4: Knit.

Rep rnds 1-4 two more times (64 sts). Then work rnd 1 on every alt rnd until 36 sts remain, ending with a straight rnd. Graft rem sts together.

TO FINISH

Weave in ends and block.

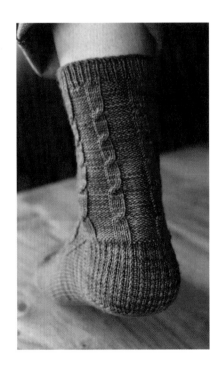

TECHNIQUES

All the skills you
need to stitch your
own socks

CASTING ON

The knitted cast on is useful because it uses many of the same moves as the knit stitch, so you can practise before you even start. The long-tail method creates a stretchier edge.

KNITTED CAST ON

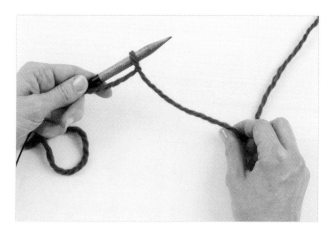

1 Start with a slipknot. Slip it on to your left-hand needle and tighten it to fit, but not so that it doesn't move easily along the needle.

2 Keeping your slipknot on the left-hand needle, insert your right-hand needle into the loop, from left to right, underneath the left-hand needle. (If it is tricky to do this, your slipknot is too tight – tug on the loop to loosen it.)

3 Bring the working yarn clockwise underneath the right-hand needle and back over the top, so you make a loop around it closer to the needle tips than the original slipknot. Use the tip of the right-hand needle to pull this new loop through the original slipknot.

4 Bring this new loop around to the tip of the left-hand needle and slip it on. You now have two stitches on the left-hand needle. To cast on more stitches, insert your right-hand needle into this new stitch and repeat steps 2–4. Repeat as many times as your pattern calls for.

TOP TIP

If you need your cast on to be stretchy, use a long-tail cast on.
If you want something firmer, try the knitted cast on.

LONG-TAIL CAST ON

1 To start a long-tail cast on, make a slipknot in your yarn, leaving a long tail of around 1in (2.5cm) for each stitch to be cast on, and slip it on to your needle.

2 With your left hand, create a slingshot shape by pointing your index finger and wrapping the working yarn clockwise over it, then raising your thumb and wrapping the tail anticlockwise over that. Curl the remaining three fingers in to grasp the yarn ends.

3 Use the needle tip to pick up the strand of yarn around the outside of your thumb, forming a loop.

4 Then pick up the strand of yarn on the inside of your index finger and pull it through the loop.

5 Let the yarn go and pull to tighten, but not too tight. You now have two stitches cast on. Repeat steps 2–5 until you have cast on the required number of stitches.

KNITTING IN THE ROUND

There are a few ways to knit in the round: you can use several double-pointed needles or a circular needle exactly the right size for your knit. The magic loop method is handy because you can use the same circular needle for any size of knitting.

1 Cast on the number of stitches you want and slide them on to the connecting cable of your circular needle.

2 Find the middle of the stitches and pull the cable out through this point, but not so far that any stitches drop off the ends of the needle tips.

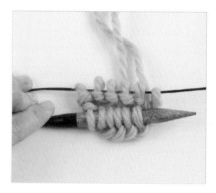

3 Leave the half of the stitches connected to the working yarn on the cable – these will be known as the back stitches. Slide the other half of the stitches on to the left-hand needle tip. These are the front stitches.

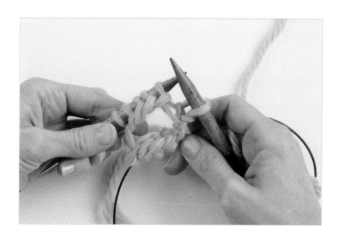

4 Bring the right-hand needle tip around and knit the first stitch on the left-hand needle tip. Pull the working yarn tightly afterwards; you will find your stitches have joined in a loop. It is a good idea to place a marker at this point so that you know where your round begins and ends.

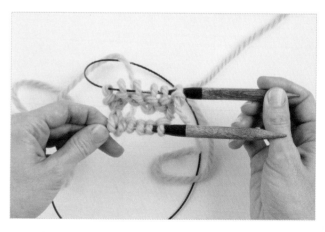

5 Carry on knitting until you have worked all the front stitches. Taking care not to flip the stitches you have worked upside down or inside out, turn the work so the stitches you have just knitted sit at the back on the left-hand needle tip and the cast-on stitches are at the front on the cable.

JOGLESS JOIN

Sometimes, joining in the round can leave a gap or irregularity that needs to be patched up at the end of the project. This simple trick is a way to avoid that and create a really neat join.

6 Pull the cable until the cast-on stitches now at the front of the work are sitting on the needle tip in front of the other needle tip. This is now your left-hand needle. Take care not to drop any stitches at this point. Pull the needle tip at the back out of the back stitches so that they sit on the cable. This is now your right-hand needle tip. Bring this needle tip around and work the first stitch on the left-hand needle. Carry on knitting until you have worked all the stitches on the needle tip. You have now knitted one round. Repeat for as many rounds as you like, creating a neat tube of knitting.

1 Cast on one more stitch than you need. Once the stitches have been distributed across your needles, slip the last cast-on stitch on to the first needle.

2 Use your fingers or a needle tip to pass the first cast-on stitch over the last cast-on stitch.

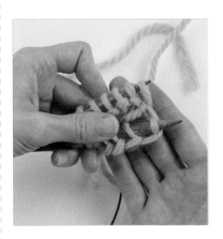

3 Now return the last cast-on stitch to its original needle. The result is a really neat, tight join.

TOP TIP

When knitting in the round, avoid ladders of loose stitches by making sure you move the gap between needles regularly. A simple way to do this is to slide the cable out so that all the stitches line up, then pull it out at a different point to continue your magic loop.

JUDY'S MAGIC CAST ON

This cast on was invented by Judy Becker, who introduced it on knitty.com.
It is a great way to start toe-up socks and other projects with an invisible, seamless base.

1 Hold two dpns (or the two tips of a circular needle if you're working with the magic loop method – see page 114) side by side. Leaving a long tail, make a slipknot and put it on the needle farther from you. This counts as your first stitch. Wrap the tail around your index finger and the working yarn around your thumb, as shown, and hold both ends in your remaining fingers.

2 Take the needle closer to you towards the yarn held by your index finger and wrap it around. It doesn't matter which way it wraps around the needle.

3 Now take the needle farther from you towards the yarn held by your thumb and wrap around. Again, it doesn't matter which way the yarn goes around the needle.

4 Repeat steps 2 and 3 until you have cast on the required number of stitches. On one side of the two rows of cast-on stitches there will be a little ridge. Make sure this ridge is facing away from you when you start knitting, so that it ends up on the inside of the sock.

5 To start knitting, hold the yarn tail tightly along the ridge of stitches. Before you work each stitch on this first round, check to see which leg is in front. If the rear leg of the stitch is in front of the front leg, knit the stitch through the back of the loop (see page 121). When the front leg of the stitch is in front, knit the stitch as normal.

WORKING WITH DPNS

If you're not used to working with double-pointed needles it looks complicated – but it's actually very easy once you get going.

1 Cast on the required number of stitches starting with one dpn and then casting on to a second. I like to cast on to two needles as I find it easier to make sure the stitches aren't twisted when joining, but you could cast on to three or four needles if you prefer.

2 Join to work in the round using the jogless join (see page 115).

3 Use a third dpn to knit the first half of the stitches on the first dpn, then bring in a fourth to knit the second half of the stitches.

4 Repeat on the second of the original two dpns, bringing in a fifth needle to knit the second half of the stitches.

5 You now have your work spread over four needles and can knit them on to the fifth needle. Simply knit one needle, then the next. I have placed a marker on the first needle so I don't forget where my round begins and ends.

TOP TIP

Some people like to move their work around the needles by a few stitches every few rounds to avoid runs of looser stitches at the gaps between dpns. I prefer to pull my working yarn tight on the first couple of stitches of each needle, and that works well for me.

KNIT STITCH

The knit stitch is the basic building block of knitting. If you can work a knit stitch, you can knit: it's that simple.

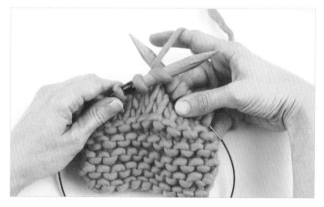

1 Hold the needle with the stitches on in your left hand and insert the tip of the right-hand needle into the first stitch, underneath the left-hand needle. The needle goes through the stitch from left to right.

2 Take the working yarn underneath and back over the right-hand needle in a clockwise direction, creating a loop in front of the stitch that is holding both needles.

3 Now use the tip of the right-hand needle to pull this loop through the original stitch.

4 The loop on your right-hand needle is the new stitch. Slip the original stitch off the end of the left-hand needle and let it fall. It now forms part of the fabric you are knitting.

5 Repeat steps 1–4 with the next stitch on the left-hand needle and then the following one until you have knitted every stitch. To knit the next row, simply turn the work around, take the right-hand needle – now with all the stitches on – in your left hand and start all over again.

PURL STITCH

The purl stitch is the mirror image of the knit stitch. All knitting patterns, no matter how complicated, are built on knit and purl stitches.

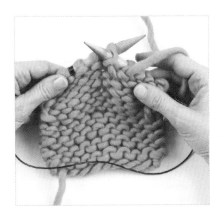

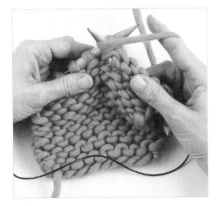

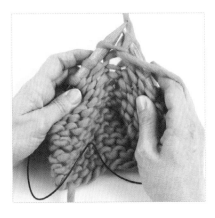

1 Insert the tip of your right-hand needle into the front of the first stitch on the left-hand needle from right to left, with the right-hand needle in front of the left-hand needle.

2 Take the working yarn clockwise underneath the right-hand needle tip and back over it, creating a new loop in front of the stitch being worked.

3 Pull the right-hand needle tip back out of the stitch, taking the new loop of yarn with it. This is now the new stitch.

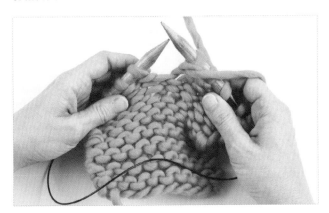

4 Let the original stitch slip off the left-hand needle to form part of the fabric.

5 Repeat steps 1–4 in the next stitch on the left-hand needle, and then the next, until all stitches have been purled. The fabric will look bobbly on the purled side and smoother on the knitted side. If you knit all the right-side rows and purl all the wrong-side rows, it is called stocking stitch – this is the most common stitch pattern you will see.

INCREASING

Increasing stitches makes your fabric wider. 'Make one left' (m1L) creates a left-slanted increase, whereas 'make one right' (m1R) creates a right-slanted increase. 'Knit front and back' (kfb) turns one stitch into two. Working increases and decreases one stitch in from the edge gives you a smooth, neat edge to your work.

MAKE ONE LEFT (M1L)

1 Knit the stitch before your increase, then find the bar that sits between this stitch and the first stitch on the left-hand needle. Insert the tip of the right-hand needle from front to back through this bar, pick it up and slip it on to the tip of the left-hand needle.

2 Knit this new stitch through the back loop (see facing page). This twists it and avoids a hole.

MAKE ONE RIGHT (M1R)

1 Find the bar before the next stitch on the right-hand needle. Insert the tip of the right-hand needle from back to front into this bar, pick it up and slip it on to the tip of the left-hand needle.

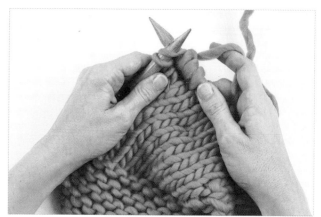

2 Knit this stitch through the front loop. This twists it and avoids a hole.

KNIT FRONT AND BACK (KFB)

1 Before you begin, take a look at the first stitch on your left-hand needle. The front of the loop (on the side of the needle facing you) should be a little in front of the back of the loop. These are also known as the front and back legs of the stitch. Start off by knitting the first stitch through its front loop as normal, but do not slip the stitch off the end of the left-hand needle.

2 Keeping the original stitch on the left-hand needle and the new stitch on the right-hand needle, take the right-hand needle tip to the back of the left-hand needle and insert it into the back loop of the original stitch.

3 Wrap the yarn around and pull the new loop through as you would in the knit stitch, then slip the original stitch off the end of the left-hand needle. You now have two stitches on the right-hand needle knitted from just one stitch on the left-hand needle.

K TBL

Knitting through the back loop can close a gap or twist a stitch to make it stand out.

Most of the time when you knit you insert the tip of the right-hand needle into the front loop of the stitch you are knitting. Inserting the needle tip into the back of the stitch, as shown here, is called 'knitting through the back loop' and twists the stitch, which can give it extra definition. Sometimes this technique is used to untwist stitches that have ended up twisted for one reason or another.

YARN OVERS

Yarn overs form the basis of lace knitting. They can be used to create decorative eyelets or as an alternative way of increasing. They work slightly differently depending on the stitch that follows and they sometimes have different names, but in this book they are all called yarn overs.

YARN OVER BEFORE A KNIT STITCH

Also known as yarn forward (yf or yfwd), yarn over needle (yon).

1 After your last stitch bring the yarn to the front of the work...

2 ...then knit the next stitch as normal, taking the working yarn over the top of the needle to the back of the work.

3 The working yarn has created a new stitch, which you can work as if it were a normal stitch on the next row.

4 This leaves a little hole in the fabric. It works in exactly the same way if you are working a knit decrease in your next stitch, even if you are slipping a stitch before you work your knit decrease. To avoid a hole, you can work the yarn over through the back loop on the next row.

TOP TIP
Yarn overs are easy to do but it can be alarming to work into such a loose stitch and to leave holes in your knitting. Just keep your cool and it will all work out fine!

YARN OVER BEFORE A PURL STITCH

Also known as yarn round needle (yrn), yarn over and round needle (yorn).

1 After your last stitch bring the yarn to the front of the needle if it isn't there already.

2 Take it over the needle to the back of the work, then bring it between the needles to the front of the work.

3 Purl the next stitch as normal.

4 On the next row, work the yarn over as if it were a normal stitch to create an eyelet, or work it through the back loop to avoid a hole. The yarn over works in the same way if you are working a purl decrease on the following stitch.

DECREASING

'Knit two together' (k2tog) is the simplest decrease and creates a right-leaning stitch. You can purl two together in a similar way. 'Slip, slip, knit' (ssk) makes a left-leaning decrease. 'Slip one, knit two together, pass slipped stitch over' (sk2po) makes a double decrease.

KNIT TWO TOGETHER (K2TOG)

1 Instead of inserting your needle into just one stitch, insert it into the next two stitches on the left-hand needle, just as if you were going to knit a single stitch. Wrap the working yarn around the needle and pull the new loop through the original two stitches.

2 Slip them off the end of the left-hand needle, just as you would if you were knitting a single stitch. You have now made two stitches into one stitch.

SLIP, SLIP, KNIT (SSK)

1 Insert the tip of the right-hand needle into the next stitch on the left-hand needle as if to knit it, but instead just slip it from the left-hand needle to the right-hand needle. Repeat with the next stitch so you have two slipped stitches on the right-hand needle.

2 Insert the left-hand needle through both those stitches from left to right in front of the right-hand needle. Wrap the working yarn around the right-hand needle, knitting the two slipped stitches together through the back loop, and slip them off the end of the left-hand needle.

SLIP ONE, KNIT TWO TOGETHER, PASS SLIPPED STITCH OVER (SK2PO)

1 Slip the next stitch from the left to the right-hand needle as if to knit.

2 Knit the following two stitches together.

3 Pass the slipped stitch over.

CABLES

Cables use an extra needle with two pointed ends called a cable needle to move stitches from one place to another. There are two basic types – with the cable needle held at the back or the front of the work – but endless variations.

CABLE FOUR FRONT (C4F)

1 Slip the next two stitches to a cable needle held at the front of the work.

2 Leaving these two stitches, knit the following two stitches as normal.

3 Now knit the two stitches on the cable needle.

4 You have created a left-leaning cable.

CABLE FOUR BACK (C4B)

1 Slip the next two stitches to a cable needle held at the back of the work.

2 Leaving these two stitches, knit the following two stitches as normal.

3 Now knit the two stitches on the cable needle.

4 You have created a right-leaning cable.

AFTERTHOUGHT HEEL

This simple technique lets you work a straight tube, then add on a heel, thumbhole or even buttonhole at the end.

1 When you come to the point where your heel is to be worked, the pattern will tell you to work a section in contrasting scrap yarn, then work the same stitches again in your main yarn. Here the sock has been cast off and you can see the scrap yarn marking the point where the heel will be.

2 Use your needle tip to pick up stitches along one side of the scrap yarn. Make sure you only pick up one leg of the stitch at a time so the needle goes right through the stitch. If you pick up the right leg of each stitch you will end up with all your stitches facing in the right direction.

3 Here is the sock with one set of stitches picked up on a double-pointed needle.

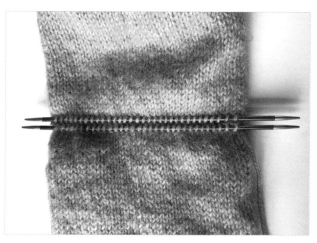

4 Once you have picked up all the stitches along one side, repeat the process on the other side of the scrap yarn.

5 Here you can see all the stitches sitting on two double-pointed needles.

6 Now carefully remove the scrap yarn from the stitches you have picked up.

7 This image shows the gap you have created, with all the stitches held safely on dpns.

8 Now pick up one or two stitches in the gaps between the two needles, according to your pattern.

9 Start knitting the stitches according to your pattern – in this case you can see I'm working in a contrast yarn.

10 This is the finished afterthought heel.

TURNING THE HEEL

A neat and handy way of turning a heel without a heel flap and gusset.

1 In this pattern the heel stitches are worked in a contrast colour. Join the new yarn neatly by working to the stitch before the heel stitches start, then working one stitch with both colour yarns held together. When you come to work this stitch, work the two shades together as one stitch.

2 In the contrast shade, knit to the last stitch of the round and wrap this stitch. In this example I am using shadow-wrap short rows (see page 132).

3 Turn the work and purl to the last heel stitch, which should be the last stitch in the contrast shade, just before the midway point marker, then wrap this stitch. Turn the work and knit to the stitch before the first wrapped stitch, then wrap this stitch.

4 Repeat on the purl side, then repeat the last two rows as many times as your pattern says. After this, knit to the first wrapped stitch – here a double stitch you can see easily – and work the wrap and wrapped stitch together. Turn.

5 Slip the stitch just worked, purl to the first wrapped stitch and purl the wrapped stitch and wrap together, then turn.

6 Slip the first stitch and repeat the last two rows until all the wraps have been worked together with their wrapped stitches, ending with a WS row. The heel is turned and you can return to working in the round.

HEEL STITCH

This slip stitch pattern gives a reinforced heel that will make your sock extra strong just where it needs it.

1 Working the heel flap always starts on the wrong side, as you turn your work after working in the round from the right side. Slip the first stitch.

2 Then purl to the end of the heel flap stitches and turn the work.

3 Now on the right side, slip the first stitch with the yarn at the back.

4 Knit the next stitch. With yarn at the back, slip the following stitch purlwise.

5 Repeat steps 3 and 4 across the row, knitting one stitch and then slipping the next purlwise with yarn at the back. End with a knit stitch.

6 These two rows are repeated to the end of the heel flap. The slip stitch pattern means you will need more rows to get the desired length than if you were working stocking stitch.

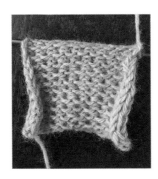

7 The result is a thicker texture with a slight rib effect on the right side, and on the wrong side the yarn across the back of the slipped stitches gives an extra layer to the heel flap.

8 The slipped stitches at each side of the heel flap let you see easily where you should pick up stitches to rejoin in the round.

HEEL FLAP AND GUSSET

Working top-down socks with a heel flap and gusset creates a more structured shape, perfect for those with high insteps.

HEEL TURN

1 After working the heel flap and the first two rows of the heel turn, knit to the last stitch before the gap, shown in this picture. Slip the stitches before and after the gap and knit them together. Knit one more stitch, then turn.

2 Work the same way on the next row, working the two stitches on either side of the gap together as p2tog. Once all stitches have been worked, knit to the end of the remaining heel stitches.

PICKING UP STITCHES

3 Place a marker here as a temporary beginning of the round. Now insert your needle tip into the first slipped stitch along the side of the heel flap, wrap the working yarn around and pull it through to pick up a stitch. Repeat with all the slipped stitches along the side of the heel flap, then pick up one more stitch in between the heel flap stitches and the instep stitches.

4 Work in pattern across the instep stitches, then start picking up stitches down the second side of the heel flap, starting with one in between the instep stitches and the first slipped stitch. I like to move my stitches around here so I have the instep and heel stitches each on one needle and the two heel flap sides on one needle each.

GUSSET

5 On the first round, work through the back loop in each of the heel flap stitches up to four stitches before the instep, then work k2tog twice. On the other side of the instep stitches, work ssk twice, then k tbl to the end of the picked-up stitches. Knit to the end of the round, then work one round straight.

6 Now work the gusset decreases as follows: on the first round, knit to the last 2 sts before the instep stitches, then work k2tog.

7 Pattern across the instep stitches, work ssk, then knit to the end of the round. You have decreased two stitches. Work the next round straight, patterning across the instep and knitting the rest of the stitches.

8 Repeat these two rows until your gusset is complete. If you have moved stitches around to accommodate the extra stitches, adjust them as necessary. Once the gusset is complete the temporary beginning of round marker should end up in the same place as the original beginning of round marker, and you can discard the temporary one.

SHADOW-WRAP SHORT ROWS

There are a number of ways to work the 'wrap and turn' used to avoid holes when shaping fabric using short rows. My favourite is the shadow-wrap method, invented by *Socktopus* author Alice Yu; this is very neat and less fiddly than some other methods.

1 Work up to the point where you are asked to wrap and turn in your pattern, then knit the stitch to be wrapped. Underneath this stitch you will notice the stitch that came before it – Alice calls this the 'mama' stitch, while the stitch on the needle is the 'daughter' stitch.

2 Lift the mama stitch on to the left-hand needle, taking care not to twist it, then knit it and drop it off. You now have two stitches on the right-hand needle, both coming out of the same mama stitch – the daughter stitch and the 'shadow' stitch.

3 Slip the stitch pair to the left-hand needle and turn to work the wrong side. Next time you come to these two stitches, you will work them together as if they were one stitch.

4 To work a shadow wrap purlwise, work to the stitch to be wrapped, then slip it purlwise on to the right-hand needle.

5 Lift the mama stitch of the slipped stitch on to the left-hand needle, being careful not to twist it, then purl it and drop the mama stitch off the needle. Once again, you have a daughter stitch and a shadow stitch coming out of the same mama stitch. Turn and work the right side. When you come to these stitches again, work them as if they were one stitch.

GERMAN SHORT ROWS

This is probably the quickest and easiest of all wraps – just note that when instructed to 'wrap and turn' you will in fact first turn, then wrap.

1 At the end of your last foot round, instead of continuing to work in the round, turn the work and, with the WS of the sole sts facing, slip the first st (the last st of the rnd) pwise.

2 Pull tightly on the working yarn so that the two legs of the stitch below the slipped stitch sit across the needle.

3 Then work the next stitch – in this case, a k st. Here you can see what looks like 3 sts on the needle, but it is actually only two: the two legs of the slipped stitch and the stitch next to them.

4 K to the end of the sole sts at the halfway point marker, turn, slip the first sole st pwise, then p the next st. Note that this heel is worked in reverse stocking stitch.

5 P to the 'wrapped' st – the one with two legs sitting across the needle, it should be easy to see – don't work it, and turn. Slip the next st pwise, then pull tightly on the working yarn as in step 2. Keep working as above as instructed by your pattern.

6 Start working the wrapped stitches beginning with a RS row. Work across the unwrapped sts and when you come to the first wrapped st, work both legs as one st, in this case p2tog.

7 Turn the work and slip the first st of the next short row.

8 K to the first wrapped st and k the two legs together.

9 Continue as set by steps 6-8 until you have worked all the wrapped sts, then get ready to continue in the round.

SHAPING A TOE-UP GUSSET

If you are working to your own design or adapting a toe-up pattern without a gusset, you will need to do some maths to work out where to start working your gusset. If you're working from a pattern, simply start where the instructions tell you to.

1 On the first round, you will place markers on either side of the heel stitches as you make your first increases. If you have not already done so, it is useful to place markers on either side of the instep stitches too, so that all four sections are clearly marked. Alternatively, as shown here, make the increases on either side of the instep markers and keep the heel stitches separate on different needles.

2 The next round is worked without increases, keeping the instep pattern correct and the sole in stocking stitch.

3 Work across the instep stitches, slip the marker and make one stitch right-leaning by inserting your needle tip into the bar between stitches from back to front, then knitting that bar through the front loop (see page 120).

4 Knit to the end of the round, slipping markers, then make one stitch left-leaning by inserting your needle tip into the bar between stitches from front to back, then knitting that bar through the back loop. Repeat steps 2-4 until you have the required number of stitches.

TOE-UP HEEL FLAP

Toe-up heel flaps are worked together with the gusset stitches as they are knitted.

1 Work to the last sole stitch. On the first couple of rows you will be working together your wrapped stitches with their wraps, as shown here. Remove the stitch marker showing where the sole and the gusset divide.

2 Work slip, slip, knit, working the last sole stitch together with the first gusset stitch. You may wish to place a marker after this stitch, but I am using my dpns to show me where I am in the pattern.

3 Turn your work and slip the stitch just worked pwise with yarn in front.

4 Purl back to the last sole stitch and remove the marker dividing sole from gusset.

5 Slip both sts to the same needle and ptog the last sole stitch with the first gusset stitch. Again, you may wish to place a marker here.

6 Turn your work, then slip the stitch you just worked pwise with yarn at the back.

7 Repeat steps 1-6 until only one gusset stitch remains on each side. Now return to working in the round. You will work the last two gusset stitches together with the sole on the first round. Knit to the last sole stitch.

8 Ssk it together with the first gusset stitch.

9 Work across the instep sts, then ktog the last gusset stitch with the first sole stitch.

10 Here you can see the neatly joined heel flap and gusset.

HELICAL STRIPES

Banish jogged stripes with this simple method, which
I learned from Arnall-Culliford Techniques.

1 After switching from the toe colour, work one round in shade A. Do not break yarn A.

2 Switch to B and knit to 3 sts before the end of the round, leaving 3 sts in A on the LH needle. Do not break B.

3 Now slip those 3 sts purlwise to the RH needle.

4 This brings the working yarn in A to the next stitch to be knitted. Pick this up and start working the next round.

5 Keep working until you come to the last 3 sts in B.

6 Slip these 3 sts purlwise to the RH needle, bringing you to the point where you left yarn B, then start working the first stitch in A with yarn B.

7 Keep repeating steps 2-6 to create a pattern of jogless helical stripes.

STRANDED COLOURWORK

Some patterns call for you to work more than one colour in the same row. In this book we strand the colour not in use behind the colour being worked in a technique sometimes known as Fairisle, after Fair Isle in Shetland, Scotland, which is famous for colourful knits using this technique.

HOLDING YARN FOR COLOURWORK KNITTING

There are two ways to hold multiple yarns when working colourwork:

- Two-handed: hold one yarn in the 'English' style in your right hand and the other in the 'continental' style in your left.

- One-handed: wind the different yarns around the same hand and pick the one you want when it comes to each stitch. You can buy knitting 'thimbles' that help keep yarns organized when working in this way.

WORKING STRANDED COLOURWORK

Most colourwork patterns are set out in a chart. Each different-coloured square represents a different stitch.

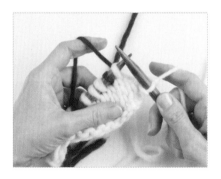

1 Work the required number of stitches in the first colour.

2 Then work the required number of stitches in the second colour.

3 The yarn not in use is stranded at the back of the fabric. To avoid long strands that may get caught on things or pull on the fabric if they end up being too tight, you need to catch the yarn not in use at regular intervals. I would recommend doing this every two or three stitches. This also helps to keep your tension even. To catch the yarn not in use, simply lift it up and take the working yarn across it as you work the next stitch.

4 This will secure it at the back of the fabric...

5 ...but won't show through at the front.

JAPANESE CLUSTER STITCH

A simple yet effective technique learned from Hitomi Shida, author of *The Japanese Knitting Stitch Bible.*

1 This pattern is based on a twisted rib, in which the knit stitches are worked tbl (see page 121) and the purl stitches are worked normally.

2 To work your cluster stitch, insert the RH needle tip pwise into the front leg of the third stitch on the LH needle.

3 Now lift the stitch over the first two stitches on the LH needle and drop it off the needle.

4 Knit the next stitch through the front loop, yarn over, then k the following st through the front loop as well. You now have 3 sts in place of the original three.

5 On the next three rows knit all 3 sts through the front loop as normal. The fabric will spread slightly here. Then work the cluster stitch again, lifting the third stitch over the first two and off the needle.

6 On the following row you can either work (k1 tbl, p1, k1 tbl), which will leave a small eyelet above your cluster stitch as shown above, or work all three stitches through the back loop for a tighter effect.

TWO-COLOUR BRIOCHE

If you've never tried brioche before, this is a great way to start. It introduces you to all the basics of brioche knitting, but is simpler than knitting two-colour brioche back and forth.

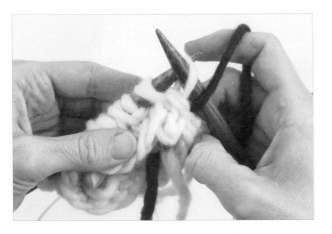

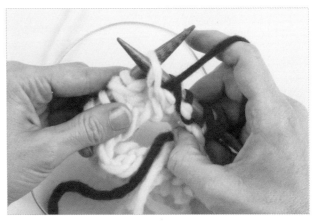

1 Using colour A, work a set-up round of (sllyo, k1). The next round is worked in B. Leaving A hanging at the back of the work, join B at the back of the work but bring it to the front to work the first stitch, which is a sllyo.

2 Using B work brp1, purling the stitch together with its yarn over. Continue to work (sllyo, brp1) around.

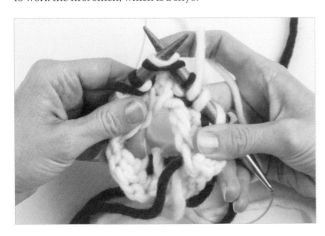

3 The next round is worked in A. Work (sllyo, brk1) around. These two rounds are repeated. The result is a lovely two-colour rib effect, with A dominant on one side and B on the other.

TWO TOE-UP SOCKS AT THE SAME TIME

Banish second sock syndrome for good by knitting two socks at the same time.

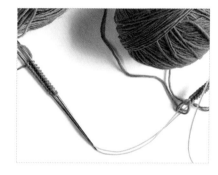

1 Start with a ball of yarn for each sock – you may have to wind off half your yarn, as shown here. You will need a circular needle with a long, flexible cable. The needles shown are HiyaHiya 2.5mm metal needles, which are strong, lightweight and flexible.

2 Start off with Judy's Magic Cast On, then slide the cast-on stitches off the needle tips on to the cable and, using your second ball of yarn, work another Judy's Magic Cast On in the same way.

3 From now on the first cast on will be known as sock A, the second as sock B. Turn the needles around ready to start knitting, with the little ridge between the two sets of stitches at the back of the work, and slide the back needle tip out of the stitches of sock B, to become your RH needle tip.

4 Bring it around ready to start knitting sock B, holding the yarn tail firmly at the back of the stitches in your left hand. Remember that on this first round you will need to untwist any twisted stitches by working them through the back loop.

5 Once you have knitted across the first side of B, slide the first set of sock A stitches on to the LH needle tip and pull the RH needle tip out of the stitches just worked so it is free to work sock A, leaving sock B on the cable.

6 At the end of the first half of sock A, slide the stitches you have just worked on to the cable so that both sets of stitches are on the cable.

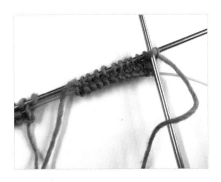

7 Turn the work, slide the second half of the A stitches on to the needle tip and bring the other needle around to start working them.

8 At the end of the second half of the A stitches, slide the second set of B stitches on to the LH needle tip and pull the RH needle tip out of the A stitches, ready to pick up yarn B and start working the B stitches.

9 Repeat steps 4-8 and follow your pattern to work the rest of the feet. When you come to the short row heels, work them one at a time, back and forth on the needles, as your pattern instructs. Then continue repeating steps 4-8 and working your leg and cuff patterns.

10 To finish, first cast off the first half of sock B, leaving one stitch on the needle. Slip this on to the cable, then cast off the first half of sock A.

11 Turn the work, slide the second half of the A stitches on to the needle tip and cast them off.

12 Once sock A has been cast off the last stitch of the first half of sock B is ready to be rejoined to the second half and the rest of the stitches cast off.

GRAFTING

Grafting allows you to join two sets of live stitches seamlessly, perfect for the toes of socks and jumper underarms.

1 This image shows two sets of live stitches at the end of an afterthought heel, held one behind the other on double-pointed needles. The stitch marker shows the beginning of the round.

2 Break the working yarn leaving a long tail and thread the end on to a large-eyed darning or tapestry needle. I have used a contrast yarn to show the steps more clearly. Insert the tapestry needle into the first stitch on the front knitting needle as if to purl, pull it through but do not drop the stitch off the needle.

3 Insert the tapestry needle into the first stitch on the back needle as if to knit, pull it through but do not drop the stitch off.

4 Now insert the tapestry needle into the first stitch on the front needle as if to knit.

5 Pull it through and drop the stitch off the needle.

6 Insert the tapestry needle into the new first stitch on the front needle as if to purl, pull it through but do not drop the stitch off the needle.

7 Insert the tapestry needle into the first stitch on the back needle as if to purl.

8 Pull it through and drop the stitch off the needle.

9 Now insert the tapestry needle into the new first stitch on the back needle as if to knit. Pull it through but do not drop it off the needle.

10 Repeat steps 4-9 until two stitches remain on the needles, then repeat steps 4, 5, 7 and 8 again. All the stitches have now been grafted using the tapestry needle. Now use the tip of the tapestry needle to tighten up any loose stitches.

11 Here you can see a neat row of contrast stitches that joins the two sections.

12 Worked in the same yarn as the knitting, the join is invisible.

CASTING OFF

Cast off your knits securely by lifting each live stitch over the next.

1 Start by working the first two stitches as normal: if it is a knit stitch, knit it; if it is a purl stitch, purl it unless your pattern says otherwise.

2 Use the tip of your left-hand needle to lift the first stitch on the right-hand needle up, over the top of the second stitch and off the end of the right-hand needle. This stitch is now cast off.

3 Knit the next stitch on the left-hand needle so that you again have two stitches on the right-hand needle, then repeat step 2.

4 Keep repeating step 3 until you have one stitch left on the right-hand needle and none on the left-hand needle. Pass the rest of the ball, or the end of the working yarn, through this last stitch, using your fingers to make the stitch big enough for the ball to fit through, then pull tightly on the working yarn. You should have a neat and tidy row of cast-off stitches.

STRETCHY CAST OFF

Toe-up socks need a stretchy cast off to sit comfortably around ankles of all sizes. This technique is super simple and very flexible.

1 Start by working the first two stitches of the row or round in pattern – in this case, knit 1, purl 1.

2 When the last stitch worked has been purl, insert the tip of the LH needle into both the worked stitches behind the RH needle and purl them together, leaving one stitch on the RH needle.

3 Work the next stitch in pattern – in this case, a knit stitch.

4 When the last stitch worked has been a knit stitch, insert the tip of the LH needle into both the worked stitches in front of the RH needle and knit the two together through the back of the loop.

5 This image shows the two stitches worked together through the back of the loop.

6 The result is a lovely stretchy cast off.

JENY'S SURPRISINGLY STRETCHY BIND OFF

This is currently my favourite stretchy cast off as it is nice and flexible but still leaves cuffs looking neat without flaring out.

1 Knit your first stitch as normal.

2 Before purling the next stitch, make a yarn over just as you normally would, from front to back and then between the needle tips to the front, ready to purl the next stitch.

3 Once you have done so, pick up both the first stitch and the yarn over with your needle tip and pass them over the last stitch worked.

4 Before a knit stitch, work a backwards yarn over: starting with the working yarn at the back, bring it towards you over the needle, then between the needle tips to the back of the work, ready to knit the next stitch.

5 Knit this stitch, then pick up both the first stitch and the yarn over with your needle tip and pass them over the last stitch worked.

6 The result is a neat but stretchy cast off.

WEAVING IN ENDS

Tidy up loose ends by weaving them into the knitting following the knitted yarn. This technique is called Swiss darning or duplicate stitch, and can also be used to embroider.

1 When you come to the end of a project, you'll have a number of ends waiting to be woven in on the wrong side of the work. Choose a large-eyed tapestry needle – blunt or sharp tips should work equally well. With the wrong side facing (in the case of a stocking-stitch project, that's the purl side), thread a yarn end through the eye of the needle. The back of the work is made up of a series of curved stitches: I will call them bowls (which dip downwards) and hats (which curve upwards). Starting with the stitch next to your loose end, insert your needle first underneath the hat next to it, then, following the stitch already running through those loops, upwards through the bowl above it on the right-hand side. Miss out the next hat, upwards and to the left of your working yarn.

2 Insert the needle downwards and to the right into the next bowl to the left of your working yarn, and then through the hat beneath and to the right of it.

3 Miss out the next bowl, then insert your needle upwards and to the right, as in step 1.

4 Repeat steps 1–3 until you have a row of stitches duplicating the stitches in the knitting and neatly securing the loose end. Keep checking your stitches aren't showing on the right side of the work.

5 Your weaving should be completely invisible on the right side, and the fabric remains nice and stretchy.

ABBREVIATIONS

k	knit	**inc**	increase
p	purl	**k2tog**	knit 2 stitches together (decrease 1)
alt	alternate	**k3tog**	knit 3 stitches together (decrease 2)
beg	begin/ning	**kfb**	knit into front and back of next stitch (increase 1)
brk1	brioche knit 1: k the next st and its yo tog	**kwise**	knitwise
brp1	brioche purl 1: p the next st and its yo tog	**kyok**	(k1, yo, k1) all into next st (increase 2)
C3B	sl2 sts to cn at back, k1, then k2 from cn	**LH**	left hand
C3F	sl1 st to cn at front, k2, then k1 from cn	**RH**	right hand
C3L	sl2 sts to cn at front, k1, k2 from cn	**m**	marker
C4B	cable 4 back: slip next 2 sts to cn at back, k2, k2 from cn	**m1**	make 1 stitch: pick up the bar between 2 sts and knit it (increase 1)
C4F	cable 4 front: slip next 2 sts to cn at front, k2, k2 from cn	**m1L**	make 1 left-leaning: pick up the bar between 2 sts from front to back, then knit it tbl (increase 1)
C4L	sl1 st to cn at front, k3, k1 from cn	**m1R**	make 1 right-leaning: pick up the bar between 2 sts from back to front, then knit into front of it (increase 1)
C4R	sl3 sts to cn at back, k1, k3 from cn		
C6B	sl3 sts to cn at back, k3, k3 from cn	**m1p**	make 1 purlwise (increase 1)
C6F	sl3 sts to cn at front, k3, k3 from cn	**m st**	moss stitch: in the round with an even number of stitches work alternate rnds as (k1, p1) and (p1, k1) so the stitches are staggered
C8Brib	cable 8 back rib: slip next 4 sts to cn at back, k1, p2, k1 from LH needle, k1, p2, k1 from cn		
C8Frib	cable 8 front rib: slip next 4 sts to cn at front, k1, p2, k1 from LH needle, k1, p2, k1 from cn	**meas**	measures
		mm	millimetre/s
C16B	sl8 sts to cn at back, (p1, k1) from LH needle 4 times, (p1, k1) from cn 4 times	**p2tog**	purl 2 stitches together (decrease 1)
		p3tog	purl 3 stitches together (decrease 2)
cl3	cluster 3 sts: insert RH needle tip into third st on LH needle and lift this over the first 2 sts and off the end of the needle, then work k1, yo, k1	**patt**	pattern
		pfb	purl into front and back of st (inc 1)
		pm	place marker
cm	centimetre/s	**psso**	pass slipped stitch over
cn	cable needle	**pwise**	purlwise
cont	continue	**rem**	remain/ing
Cr3L	cross 3 left: slip next 2 sts to cn at front, p1, k2 from cn	**rep**	repeat
		rev st st	reverse stocking stitch: when knitting back and forth work RS purl, WS knit; in the round purl every rnd
Cr3R	cross 3 right: slip next st to cn at back, k2, p1 from cn		
		rnd	round
dec	decrease	**RS/WS**	right side/wrong side
dpn(s)	double-pointed needle(s)	**skpo**	slip 1, knit 1, pass the slipped stitch over (decrease 1)
foll	follows/following	**sk2po**	slip 1, knit 2 together, pass slipped stitch over (decrease 2)
g	gramme/s		
g st	garter stitch: when knitting back and forth, knit every row; in the round work 1 rnd knit, 1 rnd purl	**sl st**	slip stitch
		sl1	slip 1 stitch
in	inch/es	**sl1p**	slip 1 stitch purlwise

sl1yo	with yarn in front slip next st pwise, take yarn over needle to the back if the next st is a k or brk st; take yarn over needle to the back then in between the tips back to the front if the next st is a p or brp st. This creates a yarn over across the slipped stitch
sm	slip marker
ssk	slip next 2 stitches one at a time, kwise, to RH needle, insert tip of LH needle through both stitches and knit them together (decrease 1)
sssk	slip, slip, slip, knit: as ssk, but with 3 sts (decrease 2)
st(s)	stitch(es)
st st	stocking stitch: when working back and forth, work RS knit, WS purl; in the round knit every rnd
tbl	through back loop
tog	together
T2	k into second st on LH needle, do not slip it off, k into first st, slip both off together

TW3	wyib, k into third st on LH needle but do not slip it off, bring yarn to front and p into the second st but do not slip it off, take yarn to back and k into back loop of first st on LH needle, then slip all 3 sts off at the same time
w&t	wrap and turn
wyib	with yarn in the back
wyif	with yarn in the front
yb	yarn back
yf	yarn forward
yo	yarn over

Work each stitch as it appears: If the next st on the left-hand needle is 'flat' (ie knitted on previous rnd) then knit this stitch, if the next stitch is a 'bump' (ie purled on previous rnd) then purl this stitch.

CONVERSIONS

The patterns in this book use UK knitting terms. Below are the translations for US terms, which are sometimes different. We also include conversion tables for knitting needle sizes.

KNITTING NEEDLE SIZES

METRIC	UK	US	METRIC	UK	US
3.5mm	9	4	6mm	4	10
4mm	8	6	6.5mm	3	10½
4.5mm	7	7	8mm	0	1
5mm	6	8	10mm	000	15
5.5mm	5	9	12mm	–	17

KNITTING AND CROCHET TERMS

UK	US
cast off	bind off
moss stitch	seed stitch
stocking stitch	stockinette stitch

SUPPLIERS

CASCADE YARNS
cascadeyarns.com

DAUGHTER OF A SHEPHERD
daughterofashepherd.com

DEBBIE BLISS
LOVECRAFTS
lovecrafts.com

EASYKNITS
easyknits.co.uk

ERIKA KNIGHT
SELECTED YARNS
erikaknight.co.uk, selected-yarns.com

GRÜNDL WOLLE
gruendl.com

HJERTEGARN
BEAUTIFUL KNITTERS
hjertegarn.dk, beautifulknitters.co.uk

JOHN ARBON
jarbon.com

MILLAMIA
LOVECRAFTS
lovecrafts.com

OPAL
VIRIDIAN YARN
viridianyarn.com

RICO
rico-design.com

ROWAN
knitrowan.com

SCHEEPJES
scheepjes.com

SWEETGEORGIA YARNS
sweetgeorgiayarns.com

THE WOOL BARN
thewoolbarn.com

THE WOOL KITCHEN
thewoolkitchen.com

WEST YORKSHIRE SPINNERS
wyspinners.com

ACKNOWLEDGEMENTS

This book is a collection of designs previously published in *Knitting* magazine, so my thanks goes out to the whole team at GMC – especially Claire Stevens who as well as designing *Knitting* and countless other beautiful magazines, has designed this book. Thanks to pattern checkers Rachel Vowles, Amelia Hodsdon and Carol Ibbetson. Big thanks to all the yarn suppliers who have offered yarn support to the magazine over the years and are featured in this book.

First published 2023 by
Guild of Master Craftsman Publications Ltd
Castle Place, 166 High Street, Lewes,
East Sussex BN7 1XU

ISBN 978 1 78494 670 8

The publishers and author can accept no legal responsibility for
any consequences arising from the application of information,
advice or instructions given in this publication.

A catalogue record for this book is available from the
British Library.

Publisher Jonathan Bailey
Production Manager Jim Bulley
Senior Project Editor Christine Boggis
Designer Claire Stevens
Proofreader Jane Roe
Technical editors Rachel Vowles, Amelia Hodsdon,
Carol Ibbetson

Colour origination by GMC Reprographics
Printed and bound in China

Picture Credits
Photographs by Laurel Guilfoyle, Christine Boggis and
Anthony Bailey
Illustrations on pages 7, 8, 9, 10 and 11 Shutterstock.com
Models Daisy Richardson, Elle Ireland

To order a book, contact:

GMC Publications Ltd,
Castle Place,
166 High Street,
Lewes, East Sussex,
BN7 1XU, United Kingdom
Tel: +44 (0)1273 488005
www.gmcbooks.com